MOUNTAIN BIKING
THE
San Gabriel Mountains'
BEST TRAILS

with
Angeles National Forest
and Mt. Pinos

By Mike Troy
and Kevin Woten

FINE EDGE
Productions

Edited by Delaine Fragnoli
Design by Sue Irwin
Photos: Mike Troy: pp. 21, 40, 61
Kevin Woten: pp. 33, 55, 120, 143, 160
Tony Quiroz: Front cover and pp. 12, 24, 30, 36, 42, 51, 53, 72, 82,
89, 96, 105, 115, 129, 152, 163, 165
Kevin Wing: Back cover

Important Disclaimer

Mountain biking is a potentially dangerous sport in which serious injury and death can and do occur. Trails have numerous natural and man-made hazards and conditions are constantly changing. Most of the routes in this book are not signed or patrolled, and this book may contain errors and omissions. It is not a substitute for proper instruction, experience, and preparedness.

The authors, editors, publisher, land managers, and others associated with this book are not responsible for errors or omissions and do not accept liability for any loss or damage incurred from using this book. You must accept full and complete responsibility for yourself while biking in the backcountry.

Library of Congress Cataloging-in-Publication Data

Troy, Mike, 1958-
     Mountain biking the San Gabriel Mountains' best trails, with
Angeles National Forest to Mt. Pinos / by Mike Troy and Kevin Woten.
        p.   cm.
     ISBN 0-938665-43-X
     1. All terrain cycling—California—San Gabriel Mountains—
Guidebooks.   2. All terrain cycling—California—Angeles National
Forest—Guidebooks.   3. Trails—California—San Gabriel Mountains—
Guidebooks.   4. Trails—California—Angeles National Forest—
Guidebooks.   5. San Gabriel Mountains (Calif.)—Guidebooks.
6. Angeles National Forest (Calif.)—Guidebooks.   I. Woten, Kevin,
1961-   .   II. Title.
GV1045.5.C22S277   1997
796.6'3'0979493—dc21   97-776
                                                              CIP

Printed in the United States of America

TABLE OF CONTENTS

Foreword

Mountain Biking the San Gabriel Mountains' Best Trails, with Angeles National Forest and Mt. Pinos covers all the best riding in Angeles National Forest: fire lookouts in the San Gabriels, high desert riding on the eastern slopes, oak woodlands in the terrain east of Castaic, and the alpine setting of Mt. Pinos, adjacent to the condor sanctuary. In this new release, which combines the best rides in two previous publications– Guide 8 (Saugus/Mt. Pinos) and Guide 9 (San Gabriel Mountains), we have updated all trail information, added new rides, and included a new series of maps, creating a comprehensive guide to mountain biking trails in this extensive region. Here are rides for after work, day-long outings, or extended weekends based from a comfortable campsite. All cyclists, from expert riders to beginners and families just starting to explore the fun of mountain biking, will benefit from the ride descriptions, anecdotes, and solid information presented by our experienced contributors.

Acknowledgments

Putting together a book like this is a formidable project, and without the support and assistance of friends and family, it would be far more difficult to accomplish. For that reason, we would like to thank the following people: John Buell, bicycle painter extraordinaire, for his assistance in the Tujunga District; all the other buddies who gave up their weekends to follow me over hill and dale–Dave Canfield, Dave Barton, Ernie Simmons, John Scobey, Troy Dennis; Stewart Penner for his help in the Valyermo District; and Paul Vautrain, singletrack magician, who showed us some of his backyard trails. The Mt. Wilson Bicycle Association for their information and good work on the trails we love to ride, and the Grapevine Mountain Bike Association, who let us drag them around the mountains while we did our research. All the fine people at the U.S. Forest Service, who took time out of their busy schedules to contribute to this book: Jim McGauley, Shawna Joyce, Don Trammel, George Geer, Greg Edwards, George Duffy, and Doug Milburn. Jerry Reynolds, Santa Clarity Valley historian, for his time and input regarding local history, and Lloyd Weins for his information on the Mt. Pinos District.

We also would like to acknowledge Mickey McTigue for permission to reprint four trail routes, and R. W. Miskimins for appendix materials.

A special thanks to Kevin Woten, who assisted in the early stages of this book and provided good company and a stalwart spirit. Kevin coauthored many rides in Chapters 9 through 13, and contributed Chapter 14, as well as Trail Canyon Trail and Red Box to Switzer in earlier chapters. Thanks also to Delaine Fragnoli, who contributed several new rides and updated trail information for the San Gabriel Mountains. She also provided helpful suggestions for improving this book. Finally, we thank our wives for being supportive and patient as we disappeared into the hills and hunched over computer screens for untold hours.

About These Rides

The following information may help you understand how we rated and measured these rides. All rides include the following information:

ROUTE/TRAIL NUMBER: When the routes are numbered, we include this information.

TRIP LENGTH (in miles): Distance is taken by a carefully calibrated cycle computer and is accurate to the best of our knowledge. Factors such as amount of portage time (time spent carrying your bike) and riding at very slow speeds can alter this. Consider the other factors when deciding on the difficulty of a ride; some 10-mile rides are more difficult than a 20-mile ride.

TIME ALLOWED: This reflects actual riding time with a small amount thrown in for good measure. Sightseeing or lunch stops are not included.

DIFFICULTY: This includes how strenuous and how technical the ride is. A very strenuous ride might include a lot of climbing or a long push or portage. A high technical rating generally relates to tight switchbacks, narrow or rocky trail footing, or a cliffside route. A fire road may have a high technical rating if it is rutted, rocky, or steep and fast. Exposed sections of trail above a cliff or steep canyon demand the utmost in skill lest you take a potentially deadly fall. Much of the singletrack in the San Gabriels is quite technical and best ridden with some experience under your belt. You'll get a feel for rating your own abilities after you've tested a few rides we have rated easy and moderate.

ELEVATION GAIN: Taken from U.S.G.S. topographical maps, this represents the major elevation gain incurred in a ride.

RIDE TYPE: The general trail surface, such as fire road (dirt, usually), trail, pavement; whether it is a loop, an out-and-back, or a shuttle ride that makes use of two vehicles.

TOPO MAP: Refers to the U.S.G.S. 7.5-minute series. We strongly advise you to carry these maps with you whenever you attempt one of the rides in this book. In addition, you should carry an Angeles National Forest map, since many of the roads and trails in the rides are shown on one map and not the other. Many trail and road numbers (e.g., 2N50) are only shown on the Forest Service map.

COMMENTS: Any other information that applies and seems pertinent at the time of this writing.

We have no doubt that in the course of putting these rides together, we have left out someone's favorite ride or perhaps included one that is sacrosanct to someone else. Many rides were not included due to the sensitive nature of the trail or problems with conflicts therein. Sorry. If, on the other hand, you know a great ride that we didn't describe, let us know. We'd like to ride it.

Special Considerations

For the beginner, the first rides in the mountains can be intimidating. But with the right attitude, a little common sense, and preparedness, you can find new adventures every weekend. We hope this book will help you along your way, but please act in a responsible manner and observe a code of behavior on the trail such as that put forth by International Mountain Bicycling Association (IMBA) in its "Rules of the Trail" (see Appendix).

If your riding is confined to city areas, you can get away without preparing for many emergency situations. But as you find yourself riding to more remote areas, you need to increase your level of preparedness. You'll be surprised how much distance you can cover on a mountain bike in a short time, and you could find yourself a long way from nowhere in a hurry!

Here are some things to keep in mind as you think about venturing off into the great unknown (or maybe just those hills behind your house!).

Part of the fun is making discoveries along the trail, so ride with your eyes wide open all the time!

1. Water. Drinking water is usually not available anywhere in the backcountry. Take all the water you will need when you do the rides described in this book. Start each trip with a minimum of 2 full water bottles, or more. Gallons of water may not be sufficient for really hot weather. Force yourself to drink, whether or not you feel thirsty. Untreated drinking water may cause giardiasis or other diseases. Carry water from a known source, or treat it.

2. Courtesy. Know and follow the IMBA Rules of the Trail. Extend courtesy to all other trail users and follow the golden rule. Yield trail to other users by stopping to exchange greetings. The trails and roads in these areas are used by fishermen, hunters, hikers, and equestrians, who all feel proprietary about the use of the trails. Mountain bikes are the newcomers here.

Get involved. Contact local bike shops and clubs that work to keep trails open and promote responsible riding.

Don't be a bad example for mountain biking. Be informed, be responsible, be safe, and enjoy the best sport in the world. But don't take my word for it: get out there and ride!

3. Preparations. Plan your trip carefully by developing a checklist. Know your abilities, your limitations, and your equipment. Prepare to be self-sufficient at all times. Bring gallons of water with you from home to save time and effort. If you plan to camp, check with the Forest Service about a permit. There's no sag wagon on the trail, and the only one who can get you back is you.

• Wear proper clothing. Helmet, gloves, and protective eyewear are a must. Good mountain biking shoes are a nice touch. Dress in layers, adding and subtracting clothing as you go so you don't overheat on climbs and freeze on the downhills. For real expeditions, take clothing for the night if necessary.

• Don't ride alone in the backcountry. You could be lying on the trail a long time before someone found you. A partner can ride for help or stay with you until help arrives. Besides the safety factor, if you're alone there's no one to see the incredible move you just pulled off crossing that 2-foot ditch! Share the fun, share the ride!

4. Mountain Conditions

• Sun: The sun in open chaparral and the higher elevations can damage your eyes, lips, and skin. Protect your skin against the sun's harmful rays. Use sunscreen with a rating of 15 or more. Don't forget your eyes! Wear sunglasses with 100 UV protection. Clear lenses are also available with 100 UV protection. Avoid glass lenses!

• Variations in temperature: Temperatures ranging from 90° to 30° F. on any given day are not uncommon in this region. Carry extra clothing—a windbreaker, gloves, stocking cap—and use the multilayer system so you can adjust according to conditions. Keep an eye on changing cloud and wind conditions.

• Fatigue. Sluggish or cramping muscles and fatigue indicate the need for calories. Carry high-energy snack foods such as granola bars, dried fruits, and nuts to maintain strength and warmth, and add clothing layers as the temperature drops or the wind increases.

• Know how to deal with dehydration, hypothermia, altitude sickness, sunburn, or heatstroke. Be sensitive at all times to the natural environment—the land can be frightening and unforgiving. If you break down, it will probably take longer to walk out than it took to ride in! Check with your local Red Cross, Sierra Club, or mountaineering textbooks for detailed survival information.

5. Horses. Many of the trails mentioned in this guide are used by recreational horse riders. Some horses are spooked easily, so make them aware of your presence well in advance of the encounter.

• If you come upon horses moving toward you, yield the right-of-way, even when it seems inconvenient. Carry your bike to the downhill

side and stand quietly, well off the trail where the animals can see you clearly. A startled horse can cause serious injuries to its rider and itself.
• If you come upon horses moving ahead of you in the same direction, stop well behind them. Do not attempt to pass until you have alerted the riders and asked for permission. Then, pass as quietly as you can on the downhill side of the trail. It is your responsibility to ensure that such encounters are safe for everyone!

6. Respect the Environment. Minimize your impact on the natural environment. Remember, you are a visitor. Due to the fragile soil conditions in Angeles National Forest, please keep a few things in mind when you ride here:
• When trails are muddy, walk your bike.
• Do not "brakeslide" your bike under any conditions.
• Leave plants.animals alone, historic and cultural sites untouched.
• Stay on established roads and trails, and do not enter private property. Follow posted instructions and use good common sense. Note: If you plan to camp within the National Forest contact the Angeles National Forest Service for information on permits, regulations and seasonal fire closures. *Remember, mountain bikes are not allowed in Wilderness Areas, on the Pacific Crest Trail and in certain other restricted areas.* Ask, when in doubt.

7. Seasonal Fire Closures and Related Hazards. Fire closures affect Angeles National Forest, particularly during summer months. Check with the USFS for any fire closures in the area you plan to visit.

In October 1993, a major fire swept across the front range of the San Gabriels. The blaze burned eastward to Kinneloa Mesa and westward to the Mt. Lowe Road, destroying several hundred homes on its way. Most of the trails in the front range were closed for weeks afterwards, and some remained closed for even longer, because soil erosion and mudslides plagued the area through the winter and spring months.

Although most trails are now open, some are subject to periodic closure because of continued landslides. The Mt. Wilson Toll Road, for example, was shut down for much of 1995 as a result of a massive landslide just above the Eaton Canyon bridge. (It took $35,000, 400 pounds of dynamite, and one very brave heavy-equipment operator to clear it.) Check with the Arroyo Seco Ranger District for trail closures. It's important to check with rangers because some roads and trails, such as the Toll Road, may not be signed closed at both ends. If you ride all the way to the bottom of the Toll Road and the gate is locked, there is no legal way out of Eaton Canyon without climbing up past Henninger Flats.

8. Control and Safety. Control your mountain bike at all times. Guard against excessive speed. Avoid overheated rims and brakes on long or steep downhill rides. Lower your center of gravity by lowering your seat on downhills. Lower your tire pressure on rough or sandy stretches. Avoid opening weekend of hunting season.

• Keep your bike in good shape. Mountain biking puts a strain on equipment, so check it often and it will be less likely to fail on the trail. Be familiar with how your bike works and how to fix it when it doesn't. When your chain breaks 10 miles out on that trail, your friendly, local bike mechanic cannot help you. Bring parts to fix your bike when it breaks, because eventually it will. Spare cables, tube, patch kit, etc., will give you that secure feeling when something goes "snap-crackle-pop" just as you reach the bottom of that canyon you've been exploring. Assemble a tool kit. A good bike shop can help you put together a kit to fit the needs of your bike. Learn to use it and always bring it with you.

9. First Aid and Safety. Carry first aid for your body as well as for your bike. If you have allergies, be sure to bring your medicine, whether it's for pollen or bee stings.

• There are black bears out and about. Food seems to cause the most frequent problems, so keep a clean camp. Rattlesnakes can be startling and are dangerous at close range, but they are usually noisy and retreat readily if given a chance. Snakes are most often seen in the lower elevations, close to a water source, hidden in the rocks. Most snake bites are reported in April, May, and early June when the snakes lie in the sun trying to warm up. Later in the summer, they hide in the shade, and you probably won't see them.

• Angeles National Forest is also home to mountain lions. In 1995 a mountain bicyclist was attacked by a lion in the general vicinity of Mt. Lowe. Although the cyclist suffered no serious injuries, the event attracted quite a bit of media attention, and a lion was eventually captured and killed. If you encounter a lion, you should make noise and try to make yourself look as big and intimidating as possible. Throw rocks or other objects. Use your bike as a shield and a weapon if necessary. No matter what, do not turn your back on a lion and do not run from it. Report all mountain lion encounters.

• Insects. Mosquitoes and deerflies are more of an annoyance than a health hazard. If the mosquitoes like you, carry insect repellant when riding, especially from May through July. Ticks are very common, so avoid contact with brush. Check your extremities periodically and remove ticks before they bury themselves in your skin.

• Avoid poison oak. Usually found in this area at 4,000 feet and below, this three-leafed plant–sometimes a bush, sometimes a vine–has an oil that causes rashes with blistering one to five days after contact. Avoid direct contact with any part of the plant, with an animal that has brushed against it, with clothing or gloves that have touched it, or inhalation of smoke from a burning plant. Wash immediately to prevent or lessen the rash. For more severe cases, see your doctor. Extremely sensitive people might check about having desensitizing shots.

• Crashes: Most crashes don't cause serious injury. Stay under control and slow down for the unexpected. Wear protective gear—helmet, full-fingered leather gloves, over-the-ankle boots, long pants, long sleeves, and dark glasses to protect against scrapes and impacts with rocks, dirt, and brush.

10. Maps & Navigation. Everyone who enjoys exploring by mountain bike should carry maps and a compass and know how to use them. The maps in this book are not designed for navigation, and they should be used with National Forest Maps and U.S. Geological Survey Maps (USGS topo maps). The handiest maps to use while riding are the USGS topo maps, 7.5 minute series, which tend to be the most recent and have many of the newer roads on them. Warning: Not all the roads on the USFS maps are on the guidebook maps, and not all the roads found on the maps in this guidebook are on the USFS maps!

It's easy to get lost. Before you leave, tell someone where you are going, when you expect to return, and what to do in case you don't return on time. Ask them to contact the County Sheriff's Department, giving full details about your vehicle and your trip plans, if you are more than six hours overdue. En route, keep track of your position on your trip map(s); record the time you arrive at a known point on the map. Look back frequently in the direction from which you came, in case you need to retrace your path. Don't be afraid to turn back when conditions change or if the going is rougher than you expected. If you find an emergency phone, dial 911.

Note: Unfortunately, some parts of the San Gabriels and Angeles National Forest, especially sections close to urban areas, are visited by folks with mischievous or destructive urges. Graffiti and vandalized property are clues to watch for. When you park your car, leave no valuables in plain sight. (Several car break-ins have been reported around the Mt. Wilson Toll Road Gate on Pinecrest Drive and at Millard Campground.) If you value your bike, don't leave it unattended.

As of this writing, all the rides in this book are legal and acceptable. This could change. If there is ever any doubt, contact the USFS for information.

Part I

The
San Gabriel
Mountains

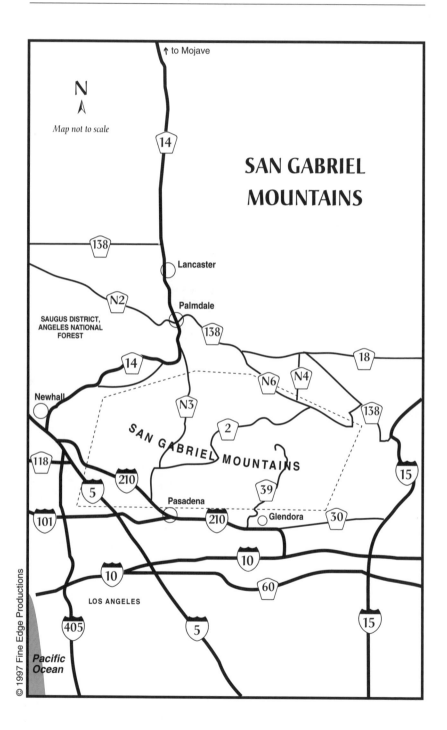

Introduction

Imagine yourself at 6,000 feet elevation in the San Gabriel Mountains, just an hour above Los Angeles, one of the largest cities in the United States. To the horizon, peak after peak of craggy mountains give way to rugged canyons. Lying west to east along the northern boundary of the Los Angeles Basin, the San Gabriels hold huge watersheds like the Big Tujunga and Big Santa Anita, which accept snowmelt of Mt. Gleason, Mt. Wilson, and Mt. Baldy, and rainfall of countless other peaks throughout the range.

For over 100 years, people have visited these mountains to seek solitude and recreation. They came first on foot, then by horse and mule or wagon; later by railroad (yes, railroad!) and automobile. Now, the rugged and sophisticated mountain bicycle can take you into the San Gabriel Mountains, providing a near-perfect vehicle for exploration and quiet, non-polluting, low impact recreation.

* * *

As the sound of labored breathing rings in your ears and mixes with a pounding of your chest, you ponder what it is that draws you here on your mountain bike.

You shift fore and aft in the saddle, gripping and re-gripping the handlebars, to try and gain a little relief. It's three more miles to the top, so you dig in, endure, and marvel at the sweat pouring off your forehead, which unerringly finds its way into your eyes before cascading off the tip of your nose.

You reach the summit, dismount, lean your bike against a rocky outcropping. Sunning lizards scatter on your presence. You take a long pull from a gritty water bottle and stand still and quiet, your heartbeat slowing as the deep breaths of clean air bring needed oxygen to your heart and lungs. The pain and suffering you endured for the past hour sweep away.

You've come to love this spot, and you ride to the top of this mountain whenever you can. When you tell people you do this for fun, they don't understand. You try to explain the sense of accomplishment, the satisfaction you feel in knowing that your own fitness and skill can take you to the top of this mountain, but it's all obscure to them. Looking around, you know why you came. As the scolding chatter of grey squirrels mixes with the rush of pine-scented breezes, some critter you never quite see skitters away through the manzanita and you forget the rush and noise of the city far below.

The San Gabriels hold something for every level of mountain cyclist. What's your preference? An easy cruise up the beautiful and historic Lower Arroyo Seco, or a 12-mile climb to the top of Mt. Gleason from the valley floor in Acton? Something in between? It's here. In time, you will grow to know these roads and trails, peaks and valleys, and someday find your favorite spot like we have. A place that rewards your toil with scenic beauty and a sense of accomplishment. . . . We hope this book will help you find that spot.

History of the San Gabriels

For centuries, people have been attracted to the canyons and summits of the San Gabriel Mountains. Native Americans established trails into and over the San Gabriels for purposes of trade. The rich resources of the area provided a bountiful living for a large population of Native Americans, and although signs of their presence in the San Gabriels are scarce today, village sites and burial grounds are scattered throughout the mountains. In the late 1700s, when the Spanish arrived–colonizing and proselytizing as they went–their influence spelled the end of Native American cultures. Many of the names in the San Gabriels and the sur-rounding cities, including the San Gabriels and the Arroyo Seco, were given by the Spanish padres. The padres' primary interest in the San Gabriels was as a source of water to support agricultural and cattle inter-ests, although they exploited the slopes of the front range to provide lumber for many of their mission buildings. In 1822, when California fell under the control of Mexico, the new governors set to dissolve the large Spanish landholdings and bequeathed large land grants to Mexi-can peoples. This era of the "ranchos" of Southern California was not to last through the eighteenth century. Encroachment of Anglo-Americans, who, in many cases, did not feel the land grants were valid, as well as periods of drought so typical of Southern California, were factors lead-ing to the decline of vast private landholdings and the thousands of cattle that roamed the lands.

In the 19th century, the San Gabriels were known as a hiding place for bandidos and horse thieves. The notorious Mexican bandit, Tiburcio Vasquez, would stage raids on the city of Los Angeles and the low-lying ranches, then disappear into the rugged canyons of the San Gabriels, frustrating many a weary posse in the twisting and difficult terrain. These outlaws shared the mountains with grizzly bears and bighorn sheep, mountain lions and the California condor. At that time, the San Gabriels were unmapped, wild country, remote, rugged, and largely unspoiled. True to our culture, we went to work changing all this.

In the mid-1800s, white men entered the San Gabriels, some fol-lowing the same trails that the early peoples had established. The first Anglos to take an interest in the San Gabriels were not nature lovers or conservation-minded citizens. Exploitation was their game. Grazing lands, mining concerns, lumber, private and public resorts, hunting and—more important than any of these—water were the key interests in opening up the San Gabriels. There were few rules and restrictions as to what one could do in the mountains. Homesteading was common in the lower canyons, and rugged individuals found retreat and a simple but successful living here. Their names live on today in places such as Brown Mountain, Sturtevants, Rubio Canyon, Colby Canyon, and Mt. Islip.

The serene beauty of many of the canyons in the front country, such as the Arroyo Seco, was an attraction to scores of people. The late 1800s and early 1900s introduced the "great hiking era" of the San Gabriels. Every weekend the trails were busy with the tramping feet of weary would-be Daniel Boones who sought solitude and exercise. Many of the trails built at the turn of the century are still in use today. Trailside resorts catering to these hikers sprang up and enjoyed great success, providing food, lodging, and fellowship for a small amount of coin—typically a dollar a night. Little of the resort era of the San Gabriels exists today. Switzer's, Oak Wilde, Martin's, Strain's, Sturtevant's, and the Mt. Lowe and Mt. Wilson hotels have disappeared. Of these places, only ghosts and cobbled foundations remain.

Game was plentiful, and Chilao and Buckhorn were popular hunting camps, arrived at by a long, tiring journey from the front country trails. Mustachioed men of rugged means established remote hunting lodges where they could hunt, fish, drink, chew, and spit, presumably without disdaining looks from womenfolk.

Mining, principally for gold and silver, underwent sporadic bursts of activity in drainages like the Big Tujunga and Big Santa Anita. Hydraulic mining—washing away the hillside with a concentrated stream of water—was popular in the San Gabriels, although it was destructive to the environment and muddied the waterways with tons of topsoil. Timbered shafts dotted the high peaks of the range, including Mt. Gleason and Mt. San Antonio. Mines with grand and hopeful names such as the Gold Dollar, Monte Christo, Big Horn, and Victoria were worked by men with visions of wealth and glory.

However, a new "mother lode" was not destined for the San Gabriels. Wild speculation and poor results were the fate of the mining camps of the 1800s, and none were successful in the long term. As late as the depression of the 1930s, men worked the washes of the San Gabriels in search of placer gold. Today the gold is still there awaiting the gold pan or dry washer of the modern prospector. (Be sure to check with the Forest Service if you are interested in prospecting. Rules and restrictions may apply.)

As cattle and sheep were brought to the mountains to graze on grasslands, fires were intentionally set to clear away the chaparral for grazing room. Incredibly destructive to the most important part of the San Gabriels–the watershed it provided for the growing communities– these immense man-made fires raged unheeded through the forest, laying waste to tens of thousands of acres.

This wanton destruction had a significant impact on forest ecology. Grizzly bears were hunted until none remained, and fish and other wild game were rapidly depleted.

Several farsighted people realized that something had to be done or little would be left for the future. In the late 1800s, Abbott Kinney, a citizen of Altadena and first chairman of California's Board of Forestry, urged the nation to preserve the mountains before all was lost. His movement gained wide support and resulted in the Forest Reserve Act of 1891, which set aside the San Gabriels as the San Gabriel Timberland Preserve (changed to the San Gabriel Forest Reserve in 1892). This act led to the establishment of the first forest rangers, whose job it was to patrol and oversee the vast reaches of the San Gabriels and to make sure the rules were followed. Early rangers were singularly rugged individuals, many of whom knew the mountains from their forays into the backcountry for hunting and exploration. Their names are familiar in the history of the San Gabriels: Delos Colby, Tom Lucas, Robert Waterman, and Louie Newcomb, among others.

As tough and resourceful as these rangers were, they lacked a professional knowledge of forestry management. In the early 1900s, men such as Theodore P. Lukens, from whom Mt. Lukens got its name, and Russ H. Charlton, of Charlton Flats fame, began to look at the San Gabriels with professional eyes and to introduce programs such as reforestation. Charlton was the first to introduce the concept of fire roads to aid in fighting wildfires. Before then, the upper reaches of the San Gabriels were hard to access, and the rugged foot trails made transport difficult for firefighters and their equipment. The extensive network of fire roads forever changed the face of the San Gabriels, but would be appreciated later by scores of forest users, including mountain bicyclists, like you and me.

Today the highways, roads, and trails that crisscross the area make visiting the forest an easy task. The grand resorts, the backcountry hunting camps, the railways, mines, and banditos have receded into the pages of history. You can ride here with little worry of encountering a grizzly bear, and that great figure in the sky above you is probably a 747, not a condor. Still, there is plenty of room for exploration and enough space to find solitude if that's what you're seeking. Many times I have stood on some timbered peak or in a shaded dell along a bubbling creek and imagined myself as one of those early San Gabriel travellers looking for the comfort of the next trail camp. You can still find that experience even in the busy crush of today's world.

And–if you still long for the forest as it was when the grizzly bear was king of the mountains, large sections of designated Wilderness have been set aside for just that reason: wildness without the intervention of modern devices. However, you will have to leave your bicycle at the boundary and proceed on foot. Don't worry, though, thousands of acres left to pedal will challenge, thrill, and reward you for years to come.

Down deep within the narrows we rode a moonlit trail, where
flashed the silver arrows, where fell a silver flail:
In dusk a dream lay hidden the while we rode along:
A melody unbidden, a half remembered song. . . .

from "The Trail Song"
by Henry Herbert Knibbs

Trail Activism in the Arroyo Seco District

The Arroyo Seco District holds a special place in the history of mountain bike trail activism. The proximity of the Angeles National Forest to the populous Los Angeles basin made it a likely place for conflicts as the sport of mountain biking began to grow in the early 1980s. In 1985, an attempt was made to close the Mt. Wilson Toll road to bicycles. To make this event even more complex, the Toll Road is the responsibility of many different public entities (note the number of padlocks on the gate). The gate and the road down to the bridge is the responsibility of the City of Pasadena and the Pasadena Water & Power Department. The Toll Road beyond the bridge up to the heliport turnoff above Henninger Flats is the domain of Los Angeles County. The Toll Road above that is in Angeles National Forest. All these groups and equestrians, hikers, and other users were brought together to resolve the conflict. Alan Armstrong represented the interests of the mountain cyclists at this meeting and helped prevent the closure of the Toll Road, thereby avoiding a precedent that would have had a catastrophic effect on the future of trail access in the area. Forming the Mt. Wilson Bicycling Association, Armstrong created the nation's first volunteer group of cyclists dedicated to maintaining and building trails on behalf of all users.

The Forest Service relies almost exclusively on volunteers to maintain the trail system. Thus, working closely with the Forest Service, the MWBA began to adopt and maintain heavily used front country trails. The group helped pioneer the use of sturdier and more effective materials for water bars and experimented with the concept of passive restraints to cue cyclists to slow down for approaching corners. The MWBA's trail work culminated with the building of the Ken Burton Trail, the first new trail in the Angeles National Forest in over 40 years and the very first to be designed and built with mountain biking in mind.

One of the most important functions of the MWBA has been to educate mountain cyclists about trail etiquette and raise awareness of the presence of other trail users. The MWBA encourages cyclists to ride and enjoy the roads and trails in the Arroyo Seco District, but urges them to ride responsibly and with the awareness that the right to continue to ride these trails has been hard won. Conflicts still arise, and the trail maintenance responsibilities of the MWBA grow every year. Everyone is invited to join an MWBA trail maintenance session; it is a fun and rewarding experience. You can reach the MWBA at (818) 795-3836.

CHAPTER 1

Mt. Baldy
and Marshall Canyon Regional Park

The Mt. Baldy District contains a significant portion of Wilderness within its boundaries. The San Gabriel, Sheep Mountain and Cucamonga Wilderness Areas restrict mountain biking possibilities since no bicycles are allowed in designated Wilderness Areas. The San Dimas Experimental Forest–closed to all National Forest users–also adds to the loss of riding area.

While Mt. San Antonio (Old Baldy) lies some distance away from these rides and is within the Wilderness Area, its impressive height makes it visible from the Sunset Peak Ride as well as from the Glendora Ridge Road.

As a mountain resort, Mt. Baldy Village, which dates back to the early 1900s, has grown along with the development of the ski area. This lovely, small mountain community, with enough permanent and weekend residents to rival Wrightwood in size, is the gateway to the Baldy Ski Area. The ski area now provides lift service to mountain bikers in the summer months, and in recent years it has hosted the Mt. Baldy Cup mountain bike races.

Lower Monroe Truck Trail

Trip Length: 14 miles
Time Allowed: 2 hours
Difficulty: Strenuous; nontechnical
Elevation Gain: 2,000'
Ride Type: Fire road out-and-back
Road Number: 2N16
Topo Map: Glendora
Comments: A popular ride in this area, the 7-mile climb is not too rugged and the downhill is superb. The road crosses the creek several times in the shaded and moist lower section near Little Dalton Picnic Area.

The ride starts at the Little Dalton picnic area, 1.5 miles up the Glendora Mountain Road from Sierra Madre Avenue in the city of Glendora. To get there, take the Azusa Avenue exit off the 210 Freeway, proceed north to Sierra Madre, and turn right. The picnic area is located to the right on a hairpin corner in the road. Parking is evident on either side of the road along the immediate area. The unmarked fire road begins just up the road from the picnic area at a locked gate.

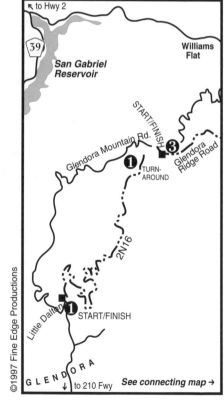

0.0 mile. The lower part of the road is really lovely and crosses the creek several times, each crossing rideable. This is a popular section with hikers, so be on the lookout. The easy grade lasts for a while until you climb out of the canyon bottom, and even then is an easy small chain ring spin all the way to the top. The last time I did this ride, it had rained the previous day and conditions were fantastic, cool and overcast, with good tacky soil and little mud. A tasty downhill follows the long climb. At 5.8 miles, keep right (straight). Soon, after a couple of big rollers, you top out at Glendora Mountain Road. Nice views into rugged canyons and up to the high peaks of the back range await on the other side of the highway. To return, you can take the Glendora Mountain Road back down to Little Dalton, but I can't imagine why you would want to. The reverse trip back down Lower Monroe Truck Trail is a hoot you shouldn't miss. Enjoy yourself but watch for other trail users, especially as you near the bottom. At 14 miles, you are back at Little Dalton.

Sunset Peak

Trip Length: 7.5 miles
Time Allowed: 90 minutes
Difficulty: Mildly strenuous; technical only in the topmost section
Elevation Gain: 1,200'
Ride Type: Fire road out-and-back
Road Number: 2N07
Topo Map: Mt. Baldy
Comments: This is a short but lovely ride and not very difficult. The many fir and oak trees along the way bid good tidings and the view from the top is outstanding.

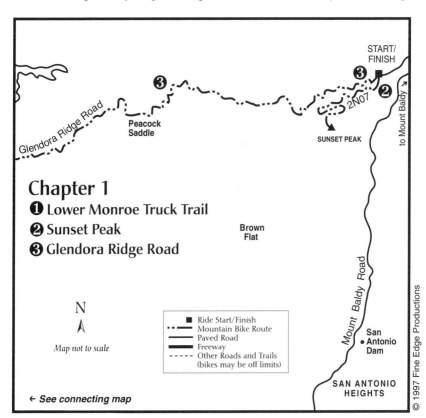

Note: This ride borders the San Dimas Experimental Forest, an area that is closed to all visitors.

From the Santa Monica Freeway (I-10) in Claremont, take the Indian Hill Boulevard exit north. Go right at Foothill and left on Mills. Take Mills to its end at Mt. Baldy Road; turn right. Soon after entering Mt. Baldy Village, look for Glendora Ridge Road—a sharp left. The ride begins off Glendora Ridge Road, 0.7 mile west of the Mt. Baldy Road at Cow Canyon Saddle. Park in the dirt lot on the north side of the road.

0.0 mile. The road to Sunset Peak takes off across the road from the parking area and past a gate. You don't have to wait long for the ride to get pretty; it already is. The grade is easy, as well. This is middle chain ring or easy small chain ring stuff, and the time passes easily. One winter day, I did this ride with patches of crusty snow still on the road and clouds all around. At one point the clouds broke and the lofty peak of Mt. San Antonio (Old Baldy), snow-capped and glistening in the sun, shone clear. Breathtaking! Even for a boy raised in hilly country, Old Baldy still is a big mountain. At 3.3 miles you ride onto a saddle. The old road to the top of Sunset Peak takes off back to the left. It is in poor repair and not easily distinguished. If you miss this turn-off and continue, you will begin to descend quickly and will soon enter the San Dimas Experimental Forest, a no-no. So if you start dropping, stop and retrace your route.

Anyway, the old road up to the peak of the mountain is rocky and technical, but passable. You may have to portage in a few places, but you can reach the peak in less than a half mile. Like many high peaks in the Angeles National Forest, there used to be a fire lookout tower here. The views into the Sheep Mountain Wilderness and the high peaks of the back range are striking and well worth the trip. To return to your vehicle, carefully retrace your steps down the mountain back to the Glendora Ridge Road.

Glendora Ridge Road

Trip Length: 12 miles one way
Time Allowed: About 2 hours round trip
Difficulty: Mildly strenuous; nontechnical
Elevation Gain: 500'
Ride Type: Out-and-back on pavement
Topo Map: Glendora, Mt. Baldy

While you usually don't think of road riding on your mountain bike, the Ridge Road is a good reason to start. Very scenic and little used by vehicles, it runs an easy course from the Glendora Mountain Road to the Mt. Baldy Road. Good pavement and small hills make this narrow road a pretty easy spin from either end, although the elevation gain goes mostly from west to east. This ride reminds me of the Old Ridge Route road from the town of Castaic, north to Highway 138 at Quail Lake (see Chapter 13). Both are mostly forgotten byways, bypassed by easier and more direct modern routes, and they both provide great bicycling. From the east end at Mt. Baldy, the parking area at Cow Canyon Saddle (see the Sunset Peak ride) is a good starting place. At the west end at the Glendora Mountain Road (see the Lower Monroe Truck Trail ride), parking is a little more obscure; any wide spot will do, but please don't block any gates or roadways.

Marshall Canyon Regional Park

Located in the foothills above the city of Claremont, Marshall Canyon Regional Park lies outside the boundaries of Angeles National Forest but still offers the mountain bicyclist fine riding in a lovely canyon environment. A small but high-quality network of roads and paths within the 4-mile-long park crisscross the area, some leading out into the National Forest. The riding here is generally mellow and is great for beginning riders and families; the more challenging and technical routes here are obvious. Expect seasonal creek crossings to add some splash to the rides. There is a good staging area located at the end of Stephens Ranch Road.

To get there, take the 210 Freeway east to its end at Foothill Bou-

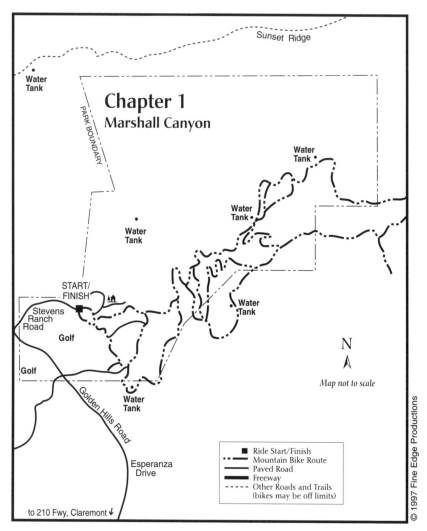

Sunset Ridge

Water Tank

PARK BOUNDARY

Chapter 1
Marshall Canyon

Water Tank

Water Tank

Water Tank

START/ FINISH

Stevens Ranch Road

Golf

Golf

Water Tank

Golden Hills Road

Water Tank

Esperanza Drive

to 210 Fwy, Claremont ↓

N
Λ

Map not to scale

■ Ride Start/Finish
▪▪▪ Mountain Bike Route
━━ Paved Road
▰▰ Freeway
----- Other Roads and Trails
(bikes may be off limits)

© 1997 Fine Edge Productions

levard. Continue on Foothill to Wheeler and go left (north). When Wheeler dead-ends at Golden Hills Road, go right. Continue to Stephens Ranch Road and turn left. Parking is on the right just before a sharp right-hand corner.

The park has been kept open to mountain bikes largely due to the efforts of concerned and active cyslists who organized–in the face of proposed trail closures–the Marshall Canyon Mounted Assistance Bike Unit. The MCMABU now patrols the park and does maintenance and cleanup on its trails. When you ride here, follow the IMBA Rules of the Trail and wave to the bike patrol folks. They deserve it!

CHAPTER 2

∂⊛

Devils Punchbowl and Big Pines
(Valyermo District)

Although this district is often passed over as desert, or forgotten completely by mountain bicyclists from the front country of the San Gabriels, it deserves better. In fact, in my opinion it contains some of the best riding in the Angeles National Forest on its relatively small network of roads and trails—and it is uncrowded, compared to well-known areas such as the Arroyo Seco. The Valyermo District is long and narrow and runs from its western border near Little Rock Reservoir to the eastern border at Wrightwood. To the north lie Valyermo and Pearblossom and the expanse of the Mojave. The San Gabriel and Sheep Mountain Wilderness Areas line its southern border.

It is the northeastern corner of the district that contains the bulk of the riding in the Valyermo, and this area is well known to snow bunnies, since it contains several ski areas. When the snow melts, the fun really begins. Beneath all that snow is a network of roads and trails through beautiful forest and thin, clean air—perfect riding conditions. While the rides are not long, they are of high quality and will keep you coming back for more. Obviously, winter is not the prime time to ride in the higher elevations, and you can expect the majority of these rides to be at their best in spring, summer, and early fall.

One of the highest peaks in the San Gabriels is contained in this district, Mt. Baden Powell at 9,399 feet. Located within the Wilderness, it is not open to bicycle travel, but offers fine, strenuous hiking. The limber pine, a variety of pine with twisted branches and needles, inhabits the summit of Mt. Baden Powell and is considered to be the oldest living thing in Angeles National Forest.

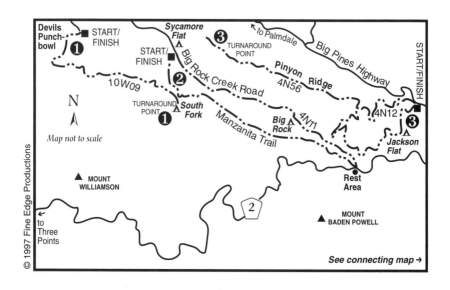

Devils Punchbowl Trail

Trip Length: 16 miles
Time Allowed: 3 hours
Difficulty: Fairly strenuous, technical
Elevation Gain: 1,500'
Ride Type: Out-and-back trail
Trail Number: 10W09
Topo Map: Valyermo
Comments: This trail runs from Devils Punchbowl County Park to the South Fork Campground and has a great time doing it. Pretty and fun to ride, a few sections are best walked. Watch for other trail users.

Take Highway 138 about 5 miles east of Little Rock to Longview Road (N6). Follow Longview to Tumbleweed Road, which turns east and becomes Longview Road again. This then becomes Devils Punchbowl Road and continues to the park–about 6 miles from Highway 138.

Devils Punchbowl County Park is located in an area of geologic interest in the juniper-covered foothills of the San Gabriels. The hike into the park itself is interesting and lovely but not the place for bikes. From the parking lot for the park, head south down a dirt road to the trailhead for two trails–the Burkhart Trail and the Punchbowl Trail. Take the east trail and head toward South Fork Campground on a good singletrack. There are two saddles to ride over before you get to

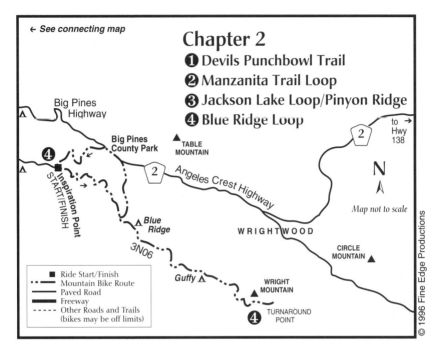

← *See connecting map*

Chapter 2
❶ Devils Punchbowl Trail
❷ Manzanita Trail Loop
❸ Jackson Lake Loop/Pinyon Ridge
❹ Blue Ridge Loop

Big Pines Highway

Big Pines County Park

❹

▲ TABLE MOUNTAIN

Inspiration Point START/FINISH

Angeles Crest Highway

2

to → Hwy 138

N

Map not to scale

© 1996 Fine Edge Productions

▲ Blue Ridge

3N06

WRIGHTWOOD

CIRCLE MOUNTAIN ▲

Guffy ▲

WRIGHT MOUNTAIN ▲

❹ TURNAROUND POINT

■ Ride Start/Finish
▪▪▪ Mountain Bike Route
── Paved Road
━━ Freeway
---- Other Roads and Trails
(bikes may be off limits)

South Fork, but this isn't too much work because it's mostly rideable. At the first saddle, Devils Chair, there is an overlook you can reach by way of a short side trail. The overlook provides a sweeping vista of the rugged canyon area of the Punchbowl and is worth the look. Back on the main trail, you descend quickly. Caution: This section of switch-backed trail is reinforced with sharp steel "landing mat" and is best walked, not ridden.

One more saddle lies between you and South Fork Campground. Climbing over this one brings you to a nice descent into South Fork. The creek has always been running when I have been through this campground, and on warm days it is a balm for hot, tired feet. As with all mountain streams in the San Gabriels, don't drink the water without treating it. There is no piped water at South Fork Campground. The trail to Islip Saddle begins out of the top of the campground and is a rugged and very exposed trip on a bicycle, steep with lots of pushing. Manzanita Trail, which begins in the lower section of the campground to the east, is much better and is described in detail in the next ride. To return to the Punchbowl, just retrace your steps on trail 10W09.

Manzanita Trail Loop

Trip Length: 13 miles
Time Allowed: 2 hours
Difficulty: Strenuous, very technical
Elevation Gain: 2,100'
Ride Type: Loop, pavement, fire road, trail
Road Number: 4N11
Topo Map: Valyermo, Crystal Lake
Comments: A very popular ride, this is a more difficult loop than either Jackson Lake or Blue Ridge. it is definitely not recommended for beginners. If you like a technical trail, then this is it.

To access this area, turn right on Longview Road from Highway 138 in the town of Pearblossom. Just 0.4 mile down Longview Road, turn left on Valyermo Road. Follow this up into the San Gabriels through the charming and tiny hamlet of Valyermo. Past the Valyermo Ranger Station, you reach the intersection with Big Rock Creek Road. Valyermo Road becomes Big Pines Highway and continues up towards Angeles Crest Highway. Turn right on Big Rock Creek Road and drive 2.1 miles, with the creek burbling along the side of the road, to the turnoff for South Fork Campground, Road 4N11. This is just a little past Sycamore Flat Campground. Find a convenient spot to park on this dirt road and begin the ride from here. Note: The gate to South Fork Camp-

ground is usually locked. Do not block access to this gate with your vehicle.

0.0 mile. Rejoin Big Rock Creek Road and turn right on the pavement. It is a quiet 3.5 mile road climb to the beginning of the dirt portion of 4N11. Just as you hit the dirt, you pass Camp Fenner, a California Department of Corrections Center. Follow the dirt road past the turnoff to Big Rock Campground and continue a steep and stutter-bumpy climb towards Vincent Gulch Divide. I don't know if this is a tough ascent, or if I was having a bad day, but this little 2-mile climb made me suffer along in the pixie ring. After a short while, at 6 miles you emerge from the maple- and oak-shaded canyon and pop out onto Angeles Crest Highway at the Vincent Gulch Divide Rest Area. Here, restrooms and a trail map of the area offer comfort and guidance to forest visitors. This is also the trailhead for Mt. Baden Powell and borders the Sheep Mountain Wilderness. Note: Be especially careful crossing Angeles Crest Highway, because it carries some fast traffic.

The trailhead for the Manzanita Trail is located on the same side of Angeles Crest Highway and just southwest of where you emerged from 4N11 onto the highway. It is marked. Lots of imprints in the trail surface attest to the popularity of this trail among all trail users. Also, the beginning of the trail is switchbacked and soft. It can be ridden without locking up your rear wheel and impacting the trail, but if you lack the skill to do so, please walk this section. Soon, you are off on a great, great trail that lets you relax for a while, then serves you a challenging little section of rocks or roots to digest.

The rest of the trail has long sections of premium singletrack in shady north-facing slopes, occasional rocky crossings in the bottom of wide drainages, and some short steep climbs. Very little pushing or carrying is required. At 10 miles or so you come to a section of trail that requires extra attention. The trail traverses a section of loose hillside. It has been reinforced with stakes and fencing, but still it is narrow and considerably exposed. Being a newcomer to clip-less pedals and feeling significantly "attached" to my bike, I walked this short section of trail. Passing some interesting outcroppings of rock, you are near the end of the trail. A few sharp switchbacks and soon you are swooping down a sandy, wriggling section of trail which drops you into South Fork Campground. The bulk of the campground is to your left and sits at the opening of the south fork of Big Rock Creek. Explore it if you wish before retracing your route down-canyon to your parked vehicle.

Jackson Lake Loop/Pinyon Ridge

Trip Length: 17 miles
Time Allowed: 2 to 3 hours
Difficulty: Mildly strenuous; strenuous if you include Pinyon Ridge; mildly technical
Elevation Gain: 2,400'
Ride Type: Loop, fire road, and trail
Topo Map: Mescal Creek, Valyermo
Comments: An easy climb if you leave out Pinyon Ridge; more challenging if you don't. A good intermediate ride with a nice singletrack return.

Begin at the Jackson Lake parking area at the turnoff to Jackson Lake, about a half-mile south of Largo Vista (N4)—or 3.5 miles past Big Rock Creek Road—on Big Pines Highway. The lake is on the south side of Big Pines Highway, and it provides a nice shady spot to stage the ride.

0.0 mile. Follow the paved entrance back out towards Big Pines Highway. Just before the highway, there is a dirt cutoff to the left. Take this path under the oaks and you come to fire road 4N12. Follow this dirt road straight ahead and up through the organization camp, rolling along an easy grade. The climb is made less stressful by the truly lovely scenery. In late September, the leaves on the big leaf maples turn auburn and red, awaiting the first cold snap to fall away and litter the ground, and the air is cool and clear. At 2.7 miles, you reach the turnoff to Pinyon Ridge. This section, of a different character, rolls along a sandy road through stands of pinyon pine and ends with a nifty view of Devils Punchbowl, although it adds to the difficulty of the ride. If you are game, turn right and climb up 4N56. The rest of you wait here, I'll be right back. The first 100 yards is the hardest section of 4N56 and is a hardscrabble grunt over the top. Then you roll along on a big rollercoaster to the end of the road, enjoying great views of the desert floor below. At 6.9 miles, the road ends and you are looking at the tortured rock formations of Devils Punchbowl County Park. The return is more difficult, as in bits and pieces, you recover the elevation you lost on the way out. At 11 miles it's back to 4N12. See, I told you I'd be back.

Continue right on 4N12 and resume the climb. At 12.3 miles, keep left at the intersection. It gets steeper for a mile or so till you get to another split in the road. The right road takes you to Angeles Crest Highway at Vincent Gulch Divide. The left road is gated. Again, stay left and continue climbing. At 13.1 miles, a trail takes off to the left. The trail starts off nicely, then soon deteriorates as it heads down to Big Pines Highway. Still, it shows promise.

Stay on Road 4N12. At about 13 miles, Angeles Crest Highway is visible to your right with Mt. Baden Powell behind. At 13.5 miles you reach a gate. Continue on. At 14 miles, Pacific Crest Trail crosses the road. *Pacific Crest Trail is not open to bicycles!* It is easy to feel the temptation to transgress, but for the sake of us all, please don't do it. Now comes the tricky part. The trail that you want to find is unmarked and is located in the shadow of a burned-out pine tree on the left of the road where a corrugated steel drainage

culvert lies to the right of the road. My computer showed 14.5 miles at the trailhead. If you arrive at Jackson Flat Campground, you have gone too far. The trail starts out tight and soon crosses Pacific Crest Trail. Again, PCT (the Pacific Coast Trail) is a no-no! The trail you are using continues downhill to the right and then continues left after crossing PCT. There is a trailside sign telling you that Jackson Lake is 2.5 miles away. This is a really good trail, although somewhat rocky, and offers more enjoyment than technical challenge. At 15.9 miles, after you plonk down a series of peeler log waterbars, you reach a road. Turn right and follow this twisty road as it dives and plunges down to Jackson Lake. Note: You are nearing several organization camps, so expect to encounter some hikers. Watch your P's and Q's.

There are several little branch roads, but by now, at 16.7 to 16.8 miles, Big Pines Highway is visible. At 16.9 miles, you reach the highway. A right turn takes you back to the Jackson Lake parking area at 17.1 miles.

Blue Ridge Loop

Trip Length: 18.5 miles
Time Allowed: 2 to 3 hours
Difficulty: Fairly strenuous, somewhat technical
Elevation Gain: 1,600'
Ride Type: Loop: pavement, fire road, trail
Road Number: 3N06
Topo Map: Mt. San Antonio, Mescal Creek
Comments: Starting and ending in the shadow of Mt. Baden Powell at Inspiration Point, this ride takes you to the doorstep of Mt. San Antonio (Old Baldy) and returns you by way of one of the finest singletracks in the forest. The trail may be omitted to make this a moderate in-and-out ride for beginners.

Begin at Inspiration Point, a scenic overlook located off Angeles Crest Highway, 2 miles west of the intersection of Angeles Crest Highway and Big Pines Highway. There is ample parking here, and a plaque located nearby gives you a guided tour of the peaks and valleys that surround you.

0.0 mile. East Blue Ridge Road, 3N06, is a paved road heading east from the parking area on the east side of the Angeles Crest Highway. It's easy to find. The road is level at first, then gradually steepens, making you work a little to continue. The slow pace up 3N06 gives you ample time to examine the many roadside flowering plants, some still in bloom in late September. You pass under some of the ski lifts of Mountain High Ski Resort before you come to Blue Ridge Campground and the end of the pavement at 2.4 miles. This is the upper trailhead of the Blue Ridge Trail. Continue on 3N06 onto the dirt. This is a lovely ride and improves as the miles pass and you distance yourself from the noise of the highway. After a short downhill, you reach the turnoff to Guffy Campground at 5.2 miles and 45 minutes or so. Stay right and continue on 3N06.

At 5.6 miles you reach another intersection. Road 3N39 drops steeply right toward Lupine and Cabin Flat Campgrounds, then ends at the Wilderness boundary. This is a 1,000-foot drop, and then there is nowhere to go by bicycle but back up the way you came. To keep pain to a minimum, bypass this and continue left on 3N06. At 7.4 miles you pass the trailhead for the Devils Backbone Trail to Mt. San Antonio. *This is not a bike trail!* Soon after, the road ends at 8.2 miles on the east side of Wright Mountain. Many small paths lead to viewpoints of the Antelope Valley and Valyermo.

When you are ready, turn around and retrace your steps to Blue

Ridge Campground. On my computer, 14.1 miles put me back at the campground and the Blue Ridge trailhead. If you opt for this trail, it will demand more uphill to return to your vehicle at Inspiration Point, but–unless you are totally fried–it's worth it. This is a great singletrack down to Angeles Crest Highway. Wide and smooth, the trail is signed as being maintained by the Wrightwood Mountain Bike Club. Good job, guys and gals!

You'll still be grinning as you reach Angeles Crest Highway at 16.3 miles. A left turn brings you to the rustic Big Pines Visitor Station, complete with restrooms and water. This old building was part of the complex that was the Big Pines County Park. In the 1920s, Los Angeles County purchased 760 acres with the intent of making a winter playground in the forest. Big Pines County Park was an immediate success, and the Forest Service extended the limits of the park to include Jackson Lake. Through the 1920s and into the 1930s, the complex grew more deluxe with skating rinks, campgrounds, and developed trails. The Great Depression of the 1930s hit hard, and the park became too much of a burden for Los Angeles County to maintain. Through the next few decades, the Forest Service gained control of the properties. Although the Big Pines area is not the deluxe mountain amusement park it once was, the natural beauty is still a draw to folks throughout the year.

To return to Inspiration Point, turn left on Angeles Crest Highway (west) and continue past Mountain High West and Big Pines Highway. After 2 miles of relatively easy pavement climbing, you are back to your starting point.

CHAPTER 3

⊗⊚

Crystal Lake Area/ Monrovia Peak

The Crystal Lake area of the San Gabriels is, in many ways, quite different from any other part of the forest. An amphitheater for nature programs, a small supply store, a visitor center, and extensive camping areas make this seem more like a national park. Contributing to this feeling are the trees—big ones; excellent stands of stately cedar trees that somehow escaped the logging that was rampant in the early days of the forest.

Having the only natural lake in the San Gabriel Mountains, the Crystal Lake area, called Pine Flat in the early years, was a haven for wildlife. According to early reports, it had more than its share of grizzlies. Hunting and vacation cabins were built in the area, and the arduous trek up from Coldbrook Camp was offset by the abundant game and beauty of the area. In the late 1920s, Los Angeles County leased land from the Forest Service and established Crystal Lake County Park. It was a huge success, and drew crowds of people seeking recreation for better than a decade. World War II ended the parade of campers driving to Crystal Lake as more prudent demands on gasoline made the long journey difficult. The area was turned over to the Forest Service to administer, which they do to this day. The Crystal Lake Store is a holdout from those bygone days, dating back to 1934.

The mountain biking in the Crystal Lake area is somewhat limited, but there is enough to keep a person busy for a camping and/or cycling weekend. This is an especially nice family camping area. There is an extensive trail system here open to mountain bikes (with the exception of the Pacific Crest Trail). However, some of the trails are not really appropriate, and they don't provide enjoyable cycling either.

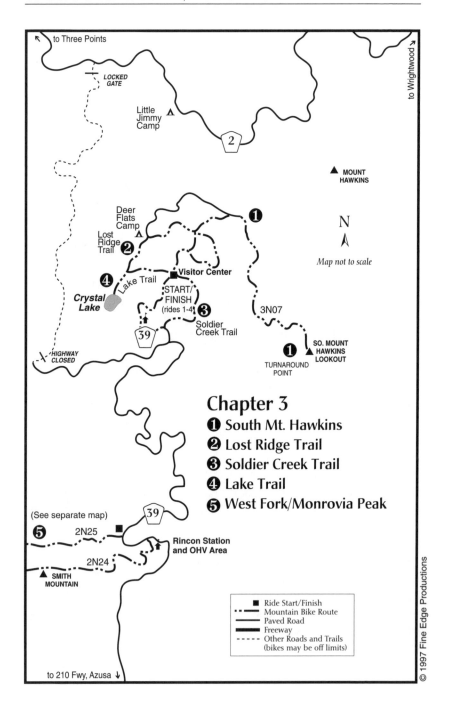

to Three Points

LOCKED
GATE

Little
Jimmy
Camp

2

to Wrightwood

▲ MOUNT
HAWKINS

Deer
Flats
Camp

❶

N
↑
Map not to scale

Lost
Ridge
Trail **❷**

Lake Trail ■ **Visitor Center**

❹

*Crystal
Lake*

START/
FINISH
(rides 1-4) **❸**

Soldier
Creek Trail

3N07

39

*HIGHWAY
CLOSED*

❶
TURNAROUND
POINT

SO. MOUNT
▲ HAWKINS
LOOKOUT

Chapter 3

❶ South Mt. Hawkins

❷ Lost Ridge Trail

❸ Soldier Creek Trail

❹ Lake Trail

❺ West Fork/Monrovia Peak

(See separate map) 39

❺ 2N25 ■

Rincon Station
and OHV Area

2N24

▲ SMITH
MOUNTAIN

■	Ride Start/Finish
▪▪▪	Mountain Bike Route
—	Paved Road
▬	Freeway
- - -	Other Roads and Trails
(bikes may be off limits)

to 210 Fwy, Azusa ↓

I feel that the ones detailed in this book are the best. In any case, please use utmost caution and observe the proper trail etiquette towards other trail users. Don't *you* be the cause of closing this area to bicyclists.

Trailhead Directions: All rides in this chapter except Monrovia Peak originate from the parking lot near the visitor center and store in the campground. From the 210 Freeway in Azusa, take Highway 39 north into the San Gabriels. Following the turnoff for Crystal Lake from Highway 39, the road into the campgrounds passes by a toll booth–where a day use or overnight fee is collected–then leads directly to the visitor center. There are area maps available here, along with program information for the campgrounds.

South Mt. Hawkins

Trip Length: 12 miles
Time Allowed: 2 hours
Difficulty: Strenuous; trail loop option adds very technical section
Elevation Gain: 1,900'
Ride Type: Fire road in and out with trail loop option
Road Number: 3N07
Topo Map: Crystal Lake
Comments: This ride takes you to the top of South Mt. Hawkins where a fire lookout tower still stands watch over the forest. (There is talk of refurbishing the tower and opening it as a visitor attraction.) There is a trail register at the top of the mountain for peakbaggers. Also, this is bighorn sheep country, so keep sharp and maybe you will see one of those rascals.

0.0 mile. From the visitor center, ride up the pavement toward the Deer Flats Campground. There is a sign at the visitor center showing this in detail. This is the main road through the campgrounds and is easy to follow. You wind along on this paved road past campsites until, at 0.4 mile, you reach the gate to Deer Flats. Ride around the gate and continue toward Deer Flats, which is reached with 0.9 mile on the computer. It gets a little steeper now but is still paved and is a very pretty ride. At 2.2 miles you come to the campground proper. There is a gated and signed (3N07) dirt road dropping off to the right of the paved road you are now on. If you miss this, you will continue into Deer Flats Campground and end up circling back around to this point anyway.

Take the dirt road and begin to climb towards South Mt. Hawkins.

The climb is never very steep—no more so than the pavement you rode to this point—but it is rocky in sections. It had been freshly graded the day I last rode it, increasing the sweat factor by 2. Soon you reach a sign that tells you you are on 3N07 and have 5 miles to the lookout, but in reality it is only 4 miles. Very near the top, the road splits. Stay right and ride the last 0.6 mile to the summit. From here you have an incredible view into the Sheep Mountain and San Gabriel Wilderness areas, down to the San Gabriel Reservoir, and to such high peaks as Mt. Wilson and Mt. Baden Powell. The trail register is located under a pile of rocks north of the lookout tower.

To head down, you can follow the fire road you came up on or take a short section of singletrack (signed Hawkins Trail) that takes off the south end of the mountain and rejoins the fire road 0.4 mile later. Either way you will head back down 3N07. At a little under 4 miles from the top of the mountain (or about 10.4 miles total), you come to where Windy Gap Trail crosses 3N07. You may have seen this on the way up. A left turn on this trail will take you down to the pavement near the visitor center. The trail return is highly recommended for the skilled rider. One thing the Crystal Lake area has a lot of (besides trees) is rocks, and this trail proves it. Bunches of rock waterbars will test your skills and make you want dual suspension in the worst way. You cross the pavement 0.7 mile into the trail and pick up the trail again on the other side. Finally, at 11.7 miles you spill out onto the pavement at the lower Windy Gap trailhead and turn right towards the visitor center. A total of 12.1 miles brings you back to your start.

Lost Ridge Trail

Trip Length: 3.2 miles
Time Allowed: 30 minutes
Difficulty: Very technical, mildly strenuous
Elevation Gain: About 800'
Ride Type: Loop, pavement-trail mix
Topo Map: Crystal Lake

0.0 mile. From the visitor center, ride the pavement toward Deer Flats Campground and turn at the gate for Deer Flats. After 1.9 miles of slight uphill, you come to the upper trailhead of the Lost Ridge Trail. There is a sign on the left marking the trailhead. This is a very technical trail in spots with some sharp switchbacks and lots of rocks to negotiate. Later, it opens up a little and is enjoyable as it winds back down through the oaks. At 2.7 miles, you intersect with the Lake Trail. Turn left to return to the visitor center. At 2.8 miles, you can cross the pavement and continue on the Lake Trail if you wish or turn left on the pavement if you have had enough rough stuff. Note: The section of the Lake Trail before you is slow and difficult, very rocky and mildly treacherous. It's a good place to take your buddy who just acquired clipless pedals and watch him flail. At 3.1 miles, you drop onto the pavement, and a left turn soon returns you to the visitor center.

Soldier Creek Trail

Trip Length: 3 miles
Time Allowed: 45 minutes to 1 hour
Difficulty: Technical, mildly strenuous
Elevation Gain: 600'
Ride Type: Loop with trail and pavement
Topo Map: Crystal Lake
Comments: Probably the best section of trail for bikes in this chapter. You follow down Soldier Creek on a narrow singletrack with enough exposure to keep you paying attention.

From the visitor center, ride toward the amphitheater. At 0.2 mile you reach the trailheads for Soldier Creek and Pinyon Ridge Trails. It's fun from the beginning, somewhat steep and, wonder of wonders, no rocks. At 0.3 mile, stay right. This is the exposed part. The trail is narrow and drops off to the left into the creek bottom. Adding to the fun is a thick carpet of oak leaves that gives a nice greased effect to the ride. At 0.8 mile you hit a split where the Soldier Creek Trail meets the Cedar Canyon Trail. Cross over the creek and continue down a short steep section of trail until you pop out onto Highway 39. Note: You may push up the Cedar Canyon Trail if you are of a mind to, but it is hard work and is too steep to ride. If you can ride up this, you are probably afraid of Kryptonite or have reeeeeal low gears. Turning right onto Highway 39 and riding uphill for 1.4 miles brings you to the entrance to the campground. A right turn here will return you to the starting point.

Lake Trail

Trip Length: 0.8 mile one way
Time Allowed: 20 minutes
Difficulty: Technical; non-strenuous
Elevation Gain: 200'
Ride Type: Trail with loop possibilities
Topo Map: Crystal Lake
Comments: This trail takes you to the namesake of the area, Crystal Lake. Varying in difficulty from section to section, this is a fun alternative to the paved road that the trail parallels.

From the visitor center, ride back down the pavement in the direction that you came into the campgrounds. Just 0.1 mile down the road, the trail takes off to the right. At 0.4 mile you cross the pavement and pick up the trail on the other side. The going is a little easier now, less rocky. You reach the end of the trail at the parking lot for the lake a nifty 0.8 mile later. A short hike down some flights of stairs leads you to the lake shore. Even when the water level is low in drought years, picnickers and fishermen still make the most of what is available. You may return by way of the trail or follow the pavement as it winds through the campgrounds back toward your starting point.

West Fork/Monrovia Peak Loop

Length: 31 miles, shorter options possible
Time: 5 to 6 hours
Difficulty: Strenuous, nontechnical
Elevation Gain: 3,500'
Ride Type: Loop on pavement and fire roads; can be done as a shorter, easier out-and-back
Road Numbers: 2N25, 2N24
Topo Maps: Glendora, Azusa, Mount Wilson
Comments: A beautiful ride, this loop travels along the scenic West Fork of the San Gabriel River before climbing over Cogswell Dam, where you have views of the San Gabriel Wilderness. The first paved part of this ride makes a nice, easy 13-mile out-and-back trip for those not up to the challenge of the whole loop.

From the 210 Freeway in Azusa, take Highway 39 north. You have to stop at the Forest Service Entrance Station on the way up and buy a parking permit, $3. Continue up the canyon about 10.5 miles from the parking kiosk, past the turnoff to the East Fork, past the OHV area, and 1.0 mile past the Rincon Ranger Station. There's a roomy parking area on your left–that's the west side of the highway. There are bathrooms and plenty of graffiti.

0.0 mile. Backtrack down the highway over the bridge. Immediately on your right, 0.1 mile, is a gated paved road (2N25), which actually looks more like a bike path. Make your way through the turnstile or over the gate.

The going is easy but you are gaining elevation, albeit very gradually. Although the first part of this ride is marred by trash and graffiti, you quickly outdistance it. Soon you have just the West Fork of the San Gabriel River and a few fishermen to keep you company.

After a mile, you pass the junction for the Bear Creek Trail. Just beyond here the river forks and you cross a bridge. You continue to parallel the West Fork until, at 1.7 miles, you cross another bridge and are back to the shady south side of the stream. Under a canopy of alder, maple, oak, and spruce, you continue to gradually gain altitude.

You pass Big Mermaids Canyon and Little Mermaids Canyon to the north (on your right). At about 4.0 miles, the canyon begins to narrow. Steep rock walls rise up on either side of you, and you pass several waterfalls trickling down mossy cliffs. If you need a restroom, there's an outhouse on the left at 4.5 miles.

At 6.5 miles you reach Glenn Trail Camp, with its sycamore-shaded picnic spaces and pit toilets (no water, however). This makes a pleasant lunch or food stop and a convenient turnaround point for those not up to the whole loop. If you have any energy left at all, though, it's worth the work to ride/push another mile up to Cogswell Dam.

To continue, saddle up and prepare to suffer. At 7.0 miles you begin a nasty little climb, still paved but very steep, to Cogswell Dam. Dedicated in 1933, the dam is named after Prescott Cogswell, a Los Angeles County Supervisor who was very involved in flood control matters. Thankfully the climb tops out at 7.5 miles. Continue on the middle route, past the private driveways (signed as such) to the left and right. It's worth your time to spin out to the dam itself and take a look up canyon on one side and down canyon on the other. To the west you can see the back of Mt. Wilson; that white dome you see is the observatory's 100-foot telescope.

From the dam, continue on the road you came in on, veering left around a switchback and past a final residence. Just beyond here at

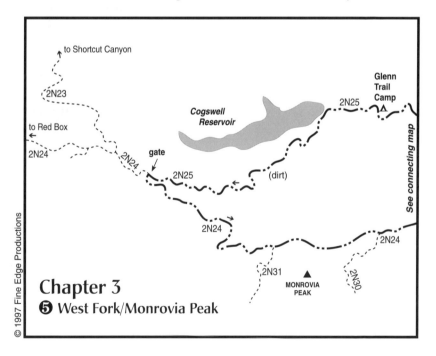

Chapter 3
❺ West Fork/Monrovia Peak

almost 8.0 miles the pavement turns to dirt. Keep climbing–and climbing and climbing–for another 6.0 miles. The grade isn't too bad, although the road surface can be shale-like in places. Thankfully, this section is generally shady, and you have views of Mt. Wilson to the west and the reservoir down below you.

At 14.0 miles you reach a gate. You've gained almost 2,000 feet since you left Glenn Trail Camp, so you deserve a break. Soak in the views and munch a Power Bar. You'll need it, because the climbing isn't quite over yet.

From the gate, make a hairpin left onto 2N24/Red Box-Rincon Road. (Had you gone right, you could take the road all the way past Newcomb Pass and up to Red Box; see Chapter 4's first ride.) At about 16.8 miles you come to gated Clamshell Road (2N31) on your right. If you want to say that you actually summited Monrovia Peak, you can take 2N31 first to Rankin Peak and then to Monrovia Peak. To do so would add roughly 5 miles and requires quite a bit of pushing. The faint trail to Rankin takes off to the left from Clamshell Road after about 1.4 miles. Be forewarned: The trail is not shown on most maps, and if you miss the turnoff, you can go for miles on Clamshell Road.

Non-peakbaggers (which is probably most of us) continue on

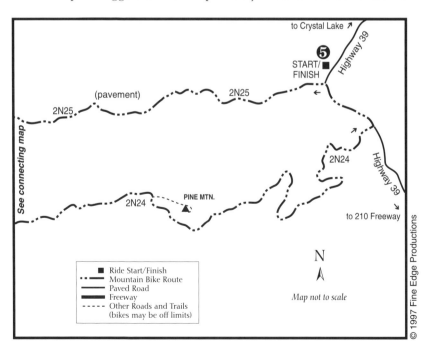

to Crystal Lake ↗

Highway 39

START/■
FINISH
5
←

(pavement)   2N25

2N25

2N24

Highway 39

to 210 Freeway

See connecting map

2N24   PINE MTN.
▲

N
Λ

Map not to scale

■ Ride Start/Finish
▪▪▪ Mountain Bike Route
━ Paved Road
━ Freeway
- - - Other Roads and Trails
(bikes may be off limits)

2N24, contouring around the north face of Monrovia Peak. Bear left at 19.2 miles when you pass gated 2N30 on your right. At 22.3 miles, veer right to avoid the turnoff (gated) to Pine Mountain (a 0.8-mile climb to the summit). Continue to head east and down, down, down—for 8 miles! This is a screaming, steep, switchbacked descent, so be careful and stay in control.

The high-speed frolic ends at 30.3 miles and the Rincon Ranger Station, where 2N24 meets Highway 39. There is a gate at the bottom of the fire road; don't go crashing into it at high speed! Turn left onto the highway for a short pavement spin, a little over half a mile, back to your waiting car.

CHAPTER 4

The Arroyo Seco Backcountry

The Arroyo Seco Backcountry is less crowded than the Front Range but is still quite popular. The extra distance from civilization yields clearer air, and the generally higher elevation provides an environment for heavy stands of pine trees instead of chaparral.

Red Box/Rincon Road with Shortcut Canyon Loop

Trip Length: 28.4 miles, but you can choose a much shorter out-and-back route
Time Allowed: 5 hours for the full ride
Difficulty: Shorter ride is strenuous but nontechnical; full ride is extremely strenuous and very, very technical
Elevation Gain: 4,600'
Ride Type: Loop, fire road, trail
Road Numbers: 2N24, 2N23
Topo Map: Mt. Wilson, Chilao Flat
Comments: Although the full loop is a monster, don't let that stop you from following part of this ride; it is a lovely and worthwhile endeavor for anyone, if done as an out-and-back ride. The West Fork of the San Gabriel River is too beautiful not to visit. Riding as far as West Fork Campground and back is a great outing of 11.2 miles round trip and is strenuous but nontechnical. For the tough among you, the entire loop is a great ride.

Take the 210 Freeway to Angeles Crest Highway (Highway 2) and head north. After you pass the junction with Angeles Forest Highway (N3), Red Box is about 4.5 miles farther, on the south side of the road. Starting from the Red Box parking lot, the Red Box Rincon Road heads east, just below the paved road to Mt. Wilson. There is a sign at the gate that reads: *Valley Forge Campground 3 Miles, West Fork Camp-*

ground 5 Miles. It's all downhill for quite a while and is very enjoyable, the road passing through deep and wooded drainages with cactus on the roadside, a strange mix indeed.

At 3.2 miles you pass Valley Forge Campground. This was the site of Valley Forge Lodge, run by the Devores, which offered good fishing, hiking, horseback riding, etc., as well as supplying the backcountry of Mt. Wilson by way of a pack train. As with many other sites, the great flood of 1938 washed away Valley Forge Camp, and it was never fully rebuilt. At 4.5 miles, you cross the creek with a splash and soon, at 5.6 miles, you reach the campground at West Fork. If you haven't noticed by now, this is really pretty country you're travelling through and this campground is especially nice. If you continue on the full ride, the singletrack section brings you back to this point. If you don't feel up to the monster loop, turn around here for the 11.2-mile ride.

To continue the loop, you need to climb out of the canyon bottom, something you'll have to do three more times. Climb past the gate in the road and head up toward Newcomb Pass. This is not a real tough climb, but it is steady and you ride uphill a few miles before topping out on the saddle at 8.8 miles. Here, at a water tank under high voltage lines, a rough trail to the right heads down to Chantry Flats. Keep straight ahead and pass the power lines on a rough fire road, now downhill somewhat, to where the road splits at 10.6 miles. To the left is a gate and the Shortcut Fire Road, 2N23. This is a mean and rocky descent back into the West Fork of the San Gabriel River. Be sure you want to go down this cuz' you don't wanna ride back up this, baby! You bottom out at 12.1 miles at one of the loveliest spots in the whole ride where the creek crosses under a concrete bridge.

A deep, still pool and the musical sounds of the water spilling over the rocks welcomes the weary cyclist. I sat eating a Power Bar and tried to imagine grizzly bears fishing in the stream for elusive trout. Years ago, the West Fork of the San Gabriel River had plenty of grizzlies and fish. It was a fisherman's delight, drawing many sportsmen to its wooded banks to try their luck. It wasn't long before overfishing and hunting had reduced the quality of the fishing and driven the grizzly from its home in the San Gabriels.

Back on the bike again, the most strenuous climb of the trip begins as the road tilts up in earnest and stays steep all the way up to Shortcut at Angeles Crest Highway. At 13.7 miles keep left. You have plenty of time to look left to Mt. Wilson and down into the canyon below before you come to the Shortcut trailhead, which takes you down into the canyon once again. The trail down Shortcut, part of the Silver Moccasin Trail, takes off left at 18.0 miles. It takes over two and a half hours of riding time to reach this point. If you are tired and can't face a difficult singletrack and the 5-mile climb to follow, you have a bail out point. The fire road continues up to Angeles Crest Highway 0.6 mile farther on. From there you could turn left and work your way back to Red Box on paved road.

If you are feeling okay, take the trail and begin a steep and challenging singletrack with tough switchbacks—some of which should be

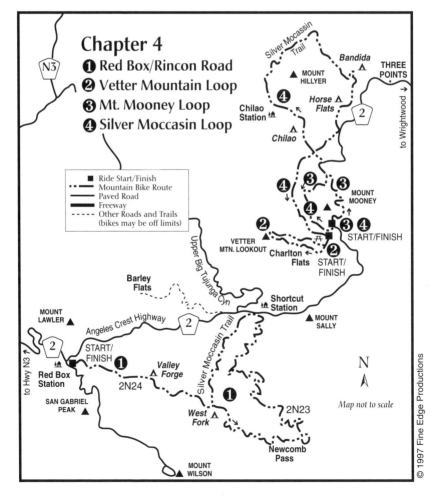

walked—and enough yucca to keep things interesting. Narrow and a little brushy on the way down, the trail changes personality completely once it hits the creek bottom. Here it winds and drops as it crosses and recrosses the creek bed over rocks, both large and small. It is a real challenge to clear as many rocks as possible without sacrificing body or bike parts to the singletrack gods. The creek crossings are tied together with sections of neat, fun trail, and are liberally sprinkled with poison oak. At 22.7 miles, the trail ends at West Fork Campground. Rest your pumped up forearms and fix any boo-boos that you might have incurred to bike or bod, and turn right on fire road 2N24. From here the ride is very straightforward with relatively easy climbing back up to Red Box. Passing by Valley Forge Campground and continuing on, one pedal stroke at a time, will surely bring you back to your starting point at the parking lot at Red Box with 28.4 miles showing on the computer.

Vetter Mountain Lookout/Trail Loop

Trip Length: 4.2+ miles
Time Allowed: 1+ hour
Difficulty: Mildly strenuous, technical
Elevation Gain: 600'
Ride Type: Loop with pavement, fire road, trail
Road Number: 3N16
Topo Map: Chilao Flat
Comments: You can be sure of two things when your destination is a Forest Service lookout tower—the climb will be a good bit of work and the view will be worth it. In this case, the climb is pretty easy compared to, say, Josephine Peak, but the view is perhaps the most enjoyable of any lookout in the forest.

It is about a 50-minute drive from Pasadena to the trailhead. From the 210 Freeway, take Angeles Crest Highway (Highway 2) north past Red Box and Shortcut stations to Charlton Flats Picnic Area on your left. Charlton Flats is the beginning of the road up to the Vetter Mountain lookout tower. You can begin anywhere in the Charlton Flats Picnic Area, but for the sake of this ride we begin at the entrance.

Ride the paved road into Charlton Flats, staying left at the first intersection and left again 0.2 mile later. After another mile, go left again and continue the short climb to the lookout on a dirt road. A rock stairway invites you to walk up and survey the forest below. When you get tired of one view (if ever), just walk around to another side of the building and gaze anew.

The return can be made a couple of ways. One is simply to backtrack the way you came. Or, there is a trail that takes off from the fire road and drops down into the lower end of the picnic area. This adds the technical rating to the ride, but is only difficult at the top and gets easier and very enjoyable nearer the bottom. To find the upper trailhead, rejoin the dirt road leading up to the lookout tower and descend 0.2 mile or so until a road turns off heading back to your left. Turn left here on this spur road. The trail drops off this road to the right and switchbacks sharply in places, most, if not all of which, can be ridden by a skilled rider. This is a great trail, very lovely and a nice challenge. Watch for hikers! You cross the pavement twice, and each time the trail continues on across the road, the going gets prettier and prettier. The trail runs out on a lower road from the picnic area, where a right turn brings you to a gate. Continuing around the gate, this paved road ends up at the entrance to the picnic area.

Note: For beginners looking for a sampling of singletrack without too much stress, it is possible to make the lower portion of the trail into a mini-loop. Starting at the gate at the lower end of the picnic area, 0.7 mile on pavement and a left turn into a small campsite hooks up to the lower section of the trail. This returns you to the pavement in short order. Good fun.

Mt. Mooney Loop

Trip Length: 3.5 miles
Time Allowed: 1 hour
Difficulty: Mildly strenuous, nontechnical
Elevation Gain: 400'
Ride Type: Loop with fire road and pavement
Topo Map: Chilao Flat, Waterman Mountain
Comments: An easy ride out of Charlton Flats, this loop does a quick jog around Mt. Mooney with a small diversion to a nearby observatory. Watch for traffic on Angeles Crest Highway.

Follow the driving directions to Charlton Flats in the previous ride. While Charlton Flats is a nice place to begin this ride, it could also be done from Chilao, 2 miles farther up the highway.

About 20 yards north of the Charlton Flats entrance, a paved road branches off to the right. Follow this road until it turns to dirt, framed by a cedar tree on the right and a pine tree on the left. This is a lovely pine-covered area, pleasant and fun to ride through. Climb for a while until, at 0.6 mile, you reach an intersection with a gated road on the right. This right road continues a short distance and ends at a small observatory.

Keeping left at 0.6 mile, you start to descend and continue to do so until you reach Angeles Crest Highway at 1.9 miles. A left turn on the highway and a little climbing for 1.5 miles returns you to Charlton Flats and your vehicle.

Silver Moccasin Loop—Charlton to Chilao

Trip Length: 13 miles
Time Allowed: 2 hours
Difficulty: Strenuous, technical
Elevation Gain: 1,000'
Ride Type: Loop, fire road, pavement, trail
Topo Map: Chilao Flat, Waterman Mountain
Comments: The trail section of Silver Moccasin Trail earns this ride the technical rating. Somewhat sandy with stair-stepped sections, Silver Moccasin is a well-used hiking trail and demands the utmost in courtesy and caution with regards to other trail users.

Follow the driving directions for the Vetter Mountain Lookout ride to Charlton Flats Picnic Area. Park at the picnic area or at the information area near the entrance to Charlton. Note: If you follow the paved

road into Charlton and keep right, you will dead-end at a gate in the roadway. This is where you will come out from Silver Moccasin Trail and it is a nice shady place to park.

0.0 mile: The entrance to Charlton Flats. Ride the 2 miles of easy pavement up Angeles Crest Highway toward Chilao Flats Campground. There are two entrances. You want to enter the lower (most southerly) one just past the Cal Trans yard located on the right (east) side of the highway.

Turn left into Chilao Flats and follow the paved road toward Manzanita Meadow Campground. At 2.4 miles, stay straight ahead, heading toward Road 3N14. At 2.8 miles, bear left. (Right leads to the visitor center.) Ride straight through the Chilao Station and at 3.7 miles, the road turns to dirt. Then it's a little tougher ride, but I had no trouble keeping it in the middle chain ring. Enjoy the climb and the view of Pacifico Mountain, Granite Mountain, and Roundtop to the northwest. At 6.2 miles turn right onto paved road. The pavement is actually steeper than the dirt road that brought you to this point. Persevere, you sweaty pilgrim, to the trailhead at 8 miles.

The Christian camp on your left is a good place to seek some shade. This was the staging area for the Angeles Crest Stage Race, a mountain bike race that used much of the roads and trails that are described in this chapter.

Across from the camp is where the Silver Moccasin Trail takes off. On the right is a gated fire road that soon dead-ends; there are also two trails, and you want to take the lower of the two. Note: This trail is heavily travelled by all trail user groups. Be a good little soldier and save the trails for all of us by not brakesliding into the corners and contributing to erosion and trail damage. There is a fork 0.5 mile down the trail near Bandido Flats Campground. Take the middle path and continue on across an abruptly steep and challenging creek crossing. Grab your granny. At 9 miles, you intersect with Horse Flats Campground. Keep left and continue down. Ka-thud, ka-thud, ka-thud goes your bike as you negotiate lots of peeler log waterbars, placed there to control erosion. Many are on blind corners in switchbacks, so be skillful or the next ka-thud may be you, not your bike.

At 10.1 miles you come to the upper road into Chilao Flats. About 100 feet or so to your left, and you pick up the trail as it drops into a wide creek bed. The trail is mellow for a while but it's all a ploy to lull your massive quads into relaxing before a really steep climb along the side of a hill. Complete with roots to cross, it does its best to hurt you. Make it up without a dab? I knew you could. At 12.2 miles, you reach the lower road into Chilao Flats. The trail picks up directly across the pavement up a short and sandy push. Soon the exact course of the trail becomes vague. Follow the trail signs to curve right and then hook left. There is more stair-step downhill, the best yet, and then the trail exits onto a fire road. Go left. This is a mean climb, but you are almost there. At 12.7 miles, you reach a gate. Go left onto the pavement and continue to Charlton Flats Picnic Area and your vehicle. Note: If you started at the entrance to Charlton at Angeles Crest Highway, follow the paved road through the picnic area and turn left at the T intersection. This will bring you out of the campground.

CHAPTER 5

The Arroyo Seco Front Range

Encompassing the front range of the San Gabriels above the foothill cities of La Canada, Altadena, and Sierra Madre, and extending northeast along Angeles Crest Highway to Krakta Ridge, the Arroyo Seco District is perhaps the most heavily used area in the San Gabriels. Angeles Crest Highway is like a magnet drawing people to the trails and camping areas easily accessed along its winding path through the mountains. Some of the most popular rides in the San Gabriels are located here. On any fair weather weekend, the Arroyo Seco up to Switzer's and Red Box, the Mt. Wilson Toll Road, Mt. Lowe, and many other popular routes bring together cyclists, hikers, and equestrians—all seeking the same benefits the forest environment supplies. The easy access and high-quality riding means you will seldom be alone as you ride. With all the heavy traffic, it's no wonder that mountain bike access in the San Gabriels became an issue here, giving birth to one of the first mountain bike trail building and land access groups—the Mt. Wilson Bicycle Association. Working with the Forest Service, the Mt. Wilson group has played a major part in keeping these areas open for our enjoyment. As you ride here, keep their efforts in mind and ride responsibly.

Mt. Lukens

Trip Length: 15 miles out-and-back, 17.4 miles with loop option
Time Allowed: 2.5 to 3 hours
Difficulty: Very strenuous, nontechnical
Elevation Gain: 2,700'
Ride Type: Loop or out-and-back on fire road
Road Number: 2N76, 2N80
Topo Map: Pasadena, Condor Peak
Comments: This is a very popular front country workout ride. The climb to the top of Mt. Lukens is a stiff one, but the view is dramatic if the air is clear enough to see any distance at all. The top of the mountain is city property and bristles with antennas instead of trees.

Mt. Lukens is named for Theodore P. Lukens, who helped shape the Angeles National Forest and introduced the concept of reforestation to the slopes of the often fire-ravaged San Gabriels. Today, electronic towers crowning the top of Mt. Lukens are the objects to aim for on this ride.

From the 210 Freeway, take Highway 2 (Angeles Crest Highway) north to the Angeles Crest Fire Station. This is not far from the city and is easily found on the left of the highway. Park near the fire station, making sure to keep your auto where it will not block any emergency vehicles.

0.0 mile. Fire road 2N76 begins at the back of the station property, so if you follow the road through the station you will come right to the fire road. The road is signed 2N76A. Up toward Mt. Lukens you go. The climb is steep in some places and is lousy with washboard from the vehicle traffic up to the electronic sites. You pass a small saddle at 1.8 miles. At 2.4 miles you come to a second saddle with a fire road coming up on your left signed for Lukens Connector Trail, Crosstown Trail, and E.T.I Corral. A half mile farther you reach a saddle.

At 3.7 miles, you intersect with the Earl Canyon motorway coming up from La Crescenta. Keep right. At 4.3 miles, keep left at the Grizzly Flat Road turnoff. It's still pretty tough climbing for a while until the road levels out a bit. At 6.3 miles, keep right. The end of the hard work is in sight, and 7.5 miles finds you at the top. The heat of the lower part of the ride is abated by a cool breeze, and there is plenty to look at if the day is clear enough—views over the valley and into the backcountry of the San Gabriels.

The return is simple if you just want to retrace your steps to Angeles Crest Station. To add some fun and mileage, make a loop out of this ride by taking the Grizzly Flat turnoff on the way down the mountain. Bounce down 2N76 from the top of Mt. Lukens until 10.6 miles brings you back to the Grizzly Flat turnoff. Turn left on 2N80 and descend a fun and twisty fire road blissfully free of washboard, but covered with loose rocks. At 12.7 miles, keep right where the road splits to drop onto Grizzly Flats. It's a little up and down until you come to a split in the road at 13.7 miles and a water tank. Angeles Crest Highway is visible below; keep right and head for it. You reach the highway at 14.4 miles. Turn right and ride back to Angeles Crest Station. This is all downhill and is an easy cruise. Keep an eye out for would-be Mario Andrettis, because the shoulder here is narrow. At 17.4 miles you are back at the start.

Hoyt Mountain

Trip Length: 8.5 miles
Time Allowed: 90+ minutes
Difficulty: Very technical, somewhat strenuous
Elevation Gain: 1,300'
Ride Type: Loop with fire road, trail, pavement
Topo Map: Condor Peak
Comments: This ride skirts around Hoyt Mountain, situated north of Angeles Crest Highway. The singletrack portion is the remains of a decaying roadbed, now narrowed into a rocky and brushy singletrack. Don't let the few nasty sections worry you though; this is still a great ride. The fire road uphill at the start is all the real climbing you do, and the fast return on Angeles Crest Highway is a fitting end. Be very aware of vehicle traffic on the highway return.
Note: Although written as a separate ride, this could easily be added to the Mt. Lukens ride to extend the length and difficulty of the trip. Riding up 2N76 toward Mt. Lukens from Angeles Crest Station to the Grizzly Flats road, 2N80, and then following 2N80 to the beginning of this ride would be a total loop of 18 miles or so and would add much more climbing. This is a great addition if you are up for the increased mileage.

Follow the driving directions for the Mt. Lukens ride, then continue 3.1 miles up Angeles Crest Highway to fire road 2N80 on the left.

0.0 mile. The road climbs up to a water tank and splits into two roads. Road 2N80 continues left toward Grizzly Flats and Mt. Lukens, but for this ride we take the right road and continue past the gate on a little-used fire road. Following power lines, this is a pretty steep climb but doesn't last long. You top out at 1.8 miles. It seems that the road ends here, but if you look past the tower on the left, there is a distinct trail heading off around the side of the mountain. The trail

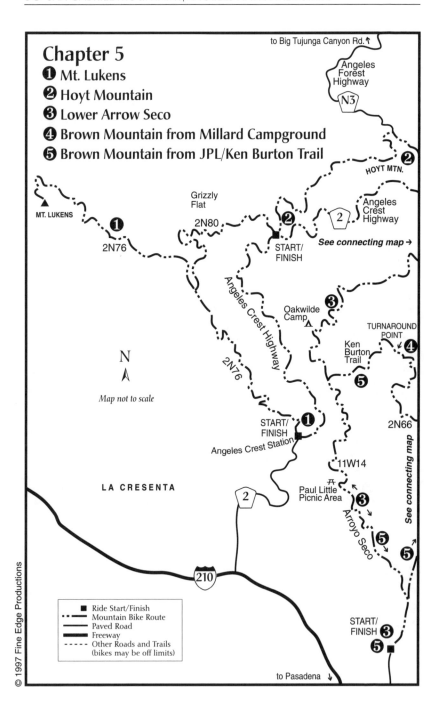

Chapter 5

❶ Mt. Lukens
❷ Hoyt Mountain
❸ Lower Arrow Seco
❹ Brown Mountain from Millard Campground
❺ Brown Mountain from JPL/Ken Burton Trail

to Big Tujunga Canyon Rd. ↑

Angeles Forest Highway

N3

MT. LUKENS

❶

2N76

Grizzly Flat

2N80

❷

HOYT MTN.

❷

2

Angeles Crest Highway

See connecting map →

START/ FINISH

Angeles Crest Highway

2N76

Oakwilde Camp

❸

Ken Burton Trail

❺

TURNAROUND POINT

❹

N ∧

Map not to scale

START/ FINISH

❶

Angeles Crest Station

2N66

See connecting map

LA CRESENTA

2

11W14

Paul Little Picnic Area

❸

Arroyo Seco

❺

❺

210

START/ FINISH ❸

❺

to Pasadena ↓

■ Ride Start/Finish
∙—∙— Mountain Bike Route
—— Paved Road
▬▬ Freeway
- - - - Other Roads and Trails
(bikes may be off limits)

© 1997 Fine Edge Productions

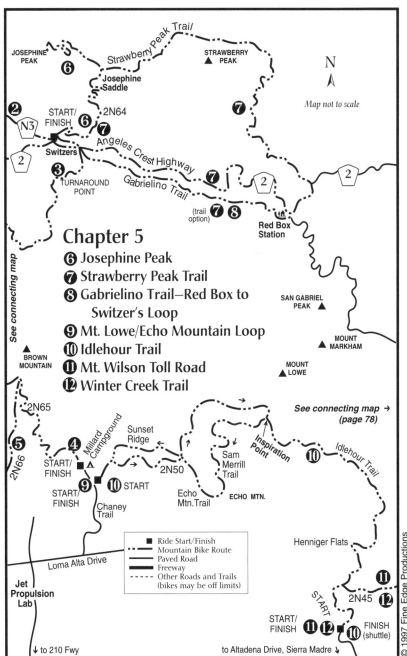

JOSEPHINE PEAK

Strawberry Peak Trail

STRAWBERRY ▲ PEAK

N

6

Josephine Saddle

2 N3

START/ FINISH **6**

2N64

7

7

Map not to scale

Angeles Crest Highway

2

Switzers

3

TURNAROUND POINT

Gabrielino Trail

7

(trail option) **7** **8**

2

2

Red Box Station

See connecting map

Chapter 5

6 Josephine Peak
7 Strawberry Peak Trail
8 Gabrielino Trail–Red Box to
   Switzer's Loop
9 Mt. Lowe/Echo Mountain Loop
10 Idlehour Trail
11 Mt. Wilson Toll Road
12 Winter Creek Trail

▲ BROWN MOUNTAIN

SAN GABRIEL PEAK ▲

MOUNT ▲ MARKHAM

MOUNT ▲ LOWE

2N65

See connecting map → (page 78)

2N66

5

START/ FINISH

4

Millard Campground

Sunset Ridge

2N50

Sam Merrill Trail

Inspiration Point

10

Idlehour Trail

START/ FINISH **9** **10** START

Chaney Trail

Echo Mtn. Trail

ECHO MTN.

Henniger Flats

11

Loma Alta Drive

Jet Propulsion Lab

■	Ride Start/Finish
─··─	Mountain Bike Route
───	Paved Road
▬▬	Freeway
----	Other Roads and Trails (bikes may be off limits)

START

2N45 **12**

START/ FINISH **11** **12** ■ **10**

FINISH (shuttle)

↓ to 210 Fwy

to Altadena Drive, Sierra Madre ↓

© 1997 Fine Edge Productions

starts out on several three-foot-deep rollers and then begins to wind its way through the rocks and brush. Except for several sections where rock slides have encroached onto the trail, this is great fun. Little yucca plants bite at your ankles and low branches swipe at your head. After a bit, the trail improves and comes to a small wooden creek crossing. Cross over this bridge and follow the road up to the pavement at the back of Clear Creek Outdoor Education Center, and turn right up the pavement. Soon you are at Angeles Forest Highway. Turn right and work your way up to Angeles Crest Highway at 4.9 miles. You are near Clear Creek Station and the road to Josephine Peak. Turn right on Angeles Crest Highway and enjoy a quick downhill all the way back to your starting point.

Lower Arroyo Seco

Trip Length: 9 to 22 miles
Time Allowed: 90 minutes to 4 hours
Difficulty: Varies in its length. Non-strenuous to strenuous and nontechnical to very technical
Elevation Gain: 2,000'
Ride Type: Out-and-back trail with loop possibilities
Topo Map: Pasadena, Condor Peak
Comments: With the exception of the Mt. Wilson Toll Road, this access is without a doubt the most well used in the front country. Due to its easy beginnings and scenic beauty, the lower Arroyo Seco is a magnet for trail users of all kinds. This trail is usually done by less experienced riders from the bottom, as far as their skills allow. The first few miles are pretty easy and very lovely. Past Oakwilde Camp, the going gets very technical and demanding. The top part of the trail pops out at Switzer's Camp and continues up-canyon to Red Box. Convenient access by auto to both the top and bottom of the trail allows an easy car shuttle and has resulted in many cyclists using the Arroyo Seco as a thrill ride, increasing tensions between cyclists and other users. The true mountain cyclist looks at the uphill as "dues" and is willing to pay them before enjoying the downhill to come. If someone in your group suggests a shuttle blitz on the Arroyo Seco, just say No!

From the Arroyo Boulevard exit on the 210 Freeway, turn left onto Windsor Avenue and drive north toward the San Gabriels for a few blocks. A good staging area is the parking lot on the left that sits above the dry wash of the Arroyo Seco across from the Jet Propulsion Lab (JPL). This parking area will nearly always be busy with cyclists gearing up for the Arroyo Seco ride.

0.0 mile. From the parking lot, ride north up Windsor Avenue to a sharp bend in the road. The road splits at this bend and goes three ways. Take the middle path around a gate where a sign announces this as part of Gabrielino National Recreational Trail, 11W14. You drop down a paved road, and at 0.7 mile, keep right. You don't have to wait long for the ride to get pretty. Ornate bridges framed with boughs of alder cross the creek, now alive with a small singing brook. The going is easy and relaxing as you travel the remains of a roadway that was placed here to serve  the resorts formerly located in the canyon. For many years, the sylvan retreats of Oakwilde and Switzer's traded upon the beauty of the Arroyo Seco to draw people to the comforts they offered.

At 1.3 miles, keep left past the Brown Mountain access road and continue up-canyon under large sycamores. Heavy rains in recent years have made the road somewhat challenging in places. You soon pass Gould Mesa Campground; then the trail gets just a touch trickier in places but is still very enjoyable.

At 3.1 miles, you pass Nino picnic grounds. Past Nino, the going gets a little more challenging, rocky and wet with stream crossings aplenty. Bounce, splash, and dab as little as possible to 4.3 miles where the trail divides at Paul Little Picnic Area. This marks a decision point. If the preceding miles were challenging enough, then this is a good stopping point. Otherwise continue up to Oakwilde. Either way, you should take a little detour to the left through Paul Little and follow a well-worn trail a short distance to the base of a nifty waterfall falling from the Brown Canyon debris dam, an especially nice snack stop.

Back on the trail split at Paul Little, if you are returning to your car, please watch your speed back down the Arroyo Seco. If you are continuing, (now at 4.7 miles if you made the detour to the waterfall) push your bike up the sandy, steep section of the Gabrielino as it climbs up along the Brown Canyon debris dam and just as quickly drops down again to creek bed level. From here to Oakwilde Camp it used to be more of the same lovely, enjoyable singletrack, just technical enough to keep an experienced rider grinning and your plebe buddies flailing. Heavy winters have taken their toll, however, and you may need to portage over areas of damaged trail. At 6.0 miles you reach Oakwilde Camp. In 1911, J. R. Phillips built a resort at this spot. Improving an old road from the mouth of the canyon to his doorstep, he made the trip to Oakwilde a possible, though adventurous, ride by auto with lots of creek crossings. The road, subject to frequent washouts, had to be rebuilt nearly every year. The resort was a great success until the great flood of 1938 washed the road away for the last time. Oakwilde Camp closed in the early 1940s. Now it's simply a nice place to rest and consider the rest of the trip.

To continue up the trail from here requires a lot more work than you put out to get to Oakwilde. In fact, unless you feel confident about your abilities and fitness, I would recommend that you turn around here and enjoy the trip down-canyon. If continuing up the trail sounds interesting but you're not sure about riding it, you do have the option of riding down it another day as part of a longer loop or shuttle of your own creation.

A lot of people would consider riding up the trail to Switzer's Camp kinda crazy. I agree and disagree. For the seasoned cyclist, this type of challenge is nearly irresistible. The section from Oakwilde to Switzer's is a small chain ring workout up a narrow and technical singletrack, often with considerable exposure. It offers little relief except the lush beauty of the canyon. Ready to go? Good. To continue on, head through Oakwilde bearing right (east) from the direction you entered the camp. The trail picks up again and begins its climb out of the shade of the canyon. Keep on trucking until at 9 miles the hard work is almost over. The trail levels out and widens, then begins descending. At 9.7 miles, keep left past the Bear Canyon Trail. Below you is Switzer's Falls. After 10 miles and several sharp switchbacks, you cross the creek to the ruins of Switzer's Camp.

Credited with being the first tourist camp in the San Gabriels, Switzer's was little more than a tent camp along the trail to Strawberry Peak, the Colby Ranch, and the Chilao backcountry. It wasn't until 1912, when Lloyd B. Austin and his wife came to this spot in the canyon, that the resort took off in a big way. Renaming the resort Switzerland, they expanded the facilities and constructed sturdy rock buildings that offered all the comforts of home among the beauty of the mountains. Switzerland drew many people–some quite famous– to its tennis courts, library, and hiking trails, and it was a popular jumping off point for travel into the backcountry.

In the 1930s foot travel into the San Gabriels declined and auto traffic increased with the new Angeles Crest Highway. As with most other resorts in the mountains, Switzerland lingered, then fell gracefully away, a casualty of a more modern age. Now all that's left are the foundations lining the canyon bottom. If you wish, you may follow the trail up-canyon 1 mile to Switzer's picnic area at Angeles Crest Highway, 11 miles and about 2 hours 30 minutes from your start.

To return, simply turn around and follow the trail back to your vehicle at Windsor Avenue for a total ride of 22 miles. Please make an effort to ride the trail softly and not brakeslide the steep sections. It is possible to ride the entire trail and never once have to lock up your rear wheel.

Brown Mountain from Millard Campground

Trip Length: 10 miles
Time Allowed: 60 to 90 minutes
Difficulty: Mildly strenuous, nontechnical
Elevation Gain: 1,200'
Ride Type: Fire road out-and-back
Road Numbers: 2N65, 2N66
Topo Map: Pasadena
Comments: This is a simple fire road ride, not too difficult, not too long, but charming nonetheless. It starts at lovely Millard Campground and ends below the summit of Brown Mountain. It is a good beginner ride.

From the 210 Freeway, take Lake Avenue north to its end at Loma Alta Drive. Go left to Chaney Trail. (There's a flashing yellow light at the intersection.) Turn right and drive up Chaney Trail to where the steep paved road splits right to Mt. Lowe and left to Millard Campground. Turn left and descend more narrow pavement to Millard. Park here.

0.0 mile. To the east of the parking lot, the Brown Mountain fire road passes through a gate and winds past lovely Millard Campground.

Millard derives its name from Henry W. Millard, who lived in the canyon in the 1800s. Shaded and cool, the road crosses a cold, gurgling stream and climbs into the sunlight, passing several private residences on the way. This steep section doesn't last long, and the rest of the ride is rolling and pretty easy. At 0.3 mile, keep right, and keep right again at 1.0 mile, 2.2 miles, and 3.7 miles. Except where a few seeps cross the road, greening things up a bit, the scenery is typical chaparral.

At 5.0 miles, the road ends at an overlook above Arroyo Seco Canyon and Angeles Crest Highway. Looming over your right shoulder is Brown Mountain, which gets its name from John Brown, the famous Civil War abolitionist. Those of you who listened in history class will remember his raid on Harper's Ferry. In the late 1800s, two of John Brown's sons, Owen and Jason, moved west and found the front country of the San Gabriels to their liking. They built a cabin near Millard Canyon, where they did some small farming and generally enjoyed their pastoral surroundings. In honor of their famous father, they christened a nearby peak Brown Mountain.

To complete the trip, simply turn around and enjoy a pleasant downhill back to Millard Campground.

Brown Mountain from JPL/ Ken Burton Trail

Trip Length: 14.8 miles
Time Allowed: 2 hours
Difficulty: Strenuous, nontechnical; singletrack option is technical
Elevation: 1,500'
Ride Type: Out-and-back on fire road; loop option with singletrack possible
Road Number: 2N66
Topo Maps: Pasadena, Condor Peak. The Ken Burton Trail is rather new and is not shown on any topo maps.
Comments: A hugely popular training ride, this trip starts at the same spot as the Arroyo Seco ride and climbs to a saddle before joining the previous ride's fire road and continuing to just below the summit of Brown Mountain. The optional singletrack return via the Ken Burton Trail to the Arroyo Seco adds a challenge for the technically adept rider. For additional details, see the Arroyo Seco ride.

Follow the directions for the Arroyo Seco ride until at 1.2 miles you reach the clearly signed Brown Mountain access road. The sign reads *Lower Brown Mountain Road, El Prieto Trail 1/4 mi, Upper Brown Mtn. Rd. 4 mi, Millard Campground 8 mi.* Go right. Stay right at the next two junctions, avoiding the private residences. You pass two trails on your right, but stay on the paved road. It crosses a stream and turns to dirt at 1.4 miles. Follow the road around a sweeping left-hand switchback and begin to climb in earnest.

At 2.0 miles you pass some green boxes on your right. Around the next corner you get your first views of the city to the south, if the air is clear. A foot trail takes off on the left at 2.2 miles; you stay on the road. You continue to climb and at 3.0 miles cross a small saddle where you have views on both sides. To your right you can see the fire road that comes up from Millard Campground, which, at 4.1 miles, intersects with the road you are riding at a large, broad saddle. This is a popular regrouping spot as well as a good turnaround point for those who have had enough climbing. Enjoy the views to the south. On a clear day you may even see the Los Angeles skyline.

From the saddle, go left and continue climbing on 2N66. After you get past the two short, steep, rocky pitches just beyond the saddle, you can relax a bit; the road levels out and even descends a little. At 4.8 miles you pass a huge oak tree. About 0.5 mile later you cross a rock slide area.

At 5.5 miles you come to a small saddle with a sign reading *Pine Spur Road 1/4 mi. Dead End.* Go right on 2N66. You begin to climb again, and at 5.7 miles you can see the road rising to a saddle ahead of you. That's your destination, and from here you have only a mile to go. You reach the top, actually a small saddle, at 6.8 miles. To the north you can see Angeles Crest Highway snaking its way across the canyon. To the south, smog permitting, you may see Los Angeles.

Those of you who prefer speed to technical challenges may turn around here and return the way you came. Control your speed because this is a heavily used route. If you like switchbacks and stream crossings, you can take the Ken Burton Trail, clearly signed at the northwest side of the saddle.

Ken Burton Trail is the first new route in the Angeles National Forest in over 40 years, and it was built by the Mount Wilson Bicycling Association (MWBA). It is also the first trail in the area to be designed with mountain biking in mind. Enjoy it, and if you want, give the MWBA a call later and offer to help maintain it. Their number is (818) 795-3836.

The narrow trail contours around a hillside, rolling pleasantly up and down. At 7.4 miles a trail on the right leads to the Ken Burton memorial. It's a pretty spot and worth a stop.

Rejoin the main trail to continue. At 8.0 miles you start a series of 20 tight switchbacks. Most are rideable for the skilled cyclist, although a few can be intimidating thanks to the trail's exposure. Some steep, loose downhills and a few rocky patches keep things interesting in between the corners.

You drop steeply toward the Arroyo Seco until the final three very steep switchbacks dump you right into a stream–literally–at 9.2 miles. You are now in the Arroyo Seco proper. Whoever named this arroyo "seco" (Spanish for "dry") was either here in a drought year or had an ironic sense of humor. You might as well portage right through the middle of the stream and get your feet wet now because you're going to get wet eventually no matter what.

Cross the stream and veer to your left. Hop the log across the trail and hook up with the Gabrielino Trail, signed at this junction. Going right will take you up the arroyo toward Switzer's. For this ride, turn left to continue the loop down the arroyo.

Ride through Oakwilde Camp at 9.3 miles. Head down the steps and straight through the stream. You have about a dozen more stream crossings to go! At 10.1 miles you begin a quarter-mile climb–steep but short. This is followed by a loose, tricky descent with switchbacks and exposure. You reach Paul Little Picnic Area at 10.4 miles.

From here it's more stream crossings, some of which you may have to portage. Be careful of the ones with big cement blocks that appear to stretch across the stream. They don't; they drop off at the far end–the perfect recipe for an endo.

The trail grows gradually wider and less technical until you're finally back on pavement. At 14.8 miles you arrive at your car on Windsor Drive.

Josephine Peak

Trip Length: 8 miles
Time Allowed: 1.5+ hours
Difficulty: Very strenuous
Elevation Gain: 1,950'
Ride Type: Fire road out-and-back
Road Number: 2N64
Topo Map: Condor Peak
Comments: This ride takes you to the top of one of the Sierra Club's 100 peaks. It is a strenuous 4-mile climb, but the view is quite spectacular. Indeed, this is one of the prettiest rides in the San Gabriels.

At the intersection of Angeles Forest Highway and Angeles Crest Highway, at Clear Creek Station, there is a parking area that makes a good place to start this ride. You can park in the dirt area at the Y of the intersection or at the information station across the highway. There will usually be other vehicles parked here, belonging to cyclists, hikers, and the like.

0.0 mile. Leave the parking area and turn onto Angeles Forest Highway (N3). Ride for 200 feet or so, then turn right on 2N64. Ride around the gate and follow the road up toward Josephine Saddle. This climb makes you feel like the Little Train That Could as you chug up one switchback after another. It is only 2.5 miles to the first summit at Josephine Saddle. Looking straight ahead to the north you can see broad-shouldered Mt. Gleason. Following east, your eyes fall away to Mill Creek Summit, then back up to Pacifico Mountain.

Turning left, continue on up toward Josephine Peak. The work isn't much easier, but it is a lot prettier once you near the top. The road dead-ends at the top and a footpath takes you to the summit proper. A trail register is hidden in a tin can under a rock pile. Sign in; you've earned it! There was a fire lookout tower on Josephine Peak but it was destroyed by fire and the foundations are all that remain. To return to your vehicle, retrace your steps down the mountain.

Strawberry Peak Trail

Trip Length: 18 miles
Time Allowed: 4 hours
Difficulty: Strenuous, very technical
Elevation Gain: 1,400'
Ride Type: Loop on fire road, trail, pavement
Topo Map: Condor Peak, Chilao Flat
Comments: This is not a trail for the inexperienced rider. There are many rough and narrow sections to negotiate, some which require portaging, although recent trail work has left the route in prime shape. This is a beautiful area and most of the trail is rideable. Some of it looks like a trials course for those warped enough to enjoy that sort of thing. *Note:* The first 2.5 miles of steep uphill is the same as the Josephine Peak ride.

At the intersection of Angeles Crest Highway and Angeles Forest Highway, by Clear Creek Ranger Station, there is room to park and begin this ride. Note: Since this is a loop, it would also be possible to start at Red Box or Switzer's Picnic Area if you prefer.

Riding north on Angeles Forest Highway from Angeles Crest Highway for 200 feet or so brings you to a gated fire road 2N64 leading off to the right. Take this steep, switchbacked road and climb 2.5 miles to Josephine Saddle. At this point, Strawberry Peak Trail leads off to the east, your right, and proceeds to wiggle its way around the backside of Strawberry Peak. Note: There is a section very near the beginning of this trail that requires portaging.

At 3 miles, the Colby Canyon Trail dives off to the right. Stay straight ahead. At 5 miles, you drop into a piney flat area beneath the dramatic sheer rock face of Strawberry Peak. This is the Strawberry Potrero. At 6 miles, you intersect with the trail to the Colby Ranch. There is a sign here that reads: *Strawberry Peak, Strawberry Potrero, and Colby Ranch.* There is also a trail register here in a metal standard on the right of the trail. Stay right toward Strawberry Peak and begin a steep climb, some of which requires pushing.

From this point on, expect to encounter more hikers, because the lower section of this trail sees more use than the upper section. In a short time, you pass by Strawberry Springs. Mossy and cool under large pines, it offers a welcome respite from the heat of the day. At 9 miles, you cross over a small ridge and bear left towards Angeles Crest Highway. The last 2 miles is really nice riding, with less brush to slap you around, and all downhill. The switchbacks and waterbars soon turn to an old roadbed and widen before dropping out onto Angeles Crest Highway across from Red Box Station. You can turn right here and ride the highway back to your starting point or take the trail from Red Box down to Switzer's Campground. The highway route is 14.6 miles round trip. For details on the trail return option, see text of the Gabrielino Trail, which follows.

Gabrielino Trail—Red Box to Switzer's Loop

Trip Length: 8.9 miles
Time Allowed: 2 hours
Difficulty: Moderately strenuous, technical in parts
Elevation Gain: 1,500'
Ride Type: Loop with singletrack and pavement
Topo Map: Chilao, Condor Peak
Comments: One of the most highly used trails in this part of the forest, this section of the Gabrielino Trail is a good primer for beginning mountain cyclists looking to experience singletrack, and it still offers much to the wizened veteran. Access to the trail at both ends allows an easy car shuttle. Unfortunately, this fact has created a ride often done as a "bombing run" by discourteous (e.g., brain dead) cyclists. No matter how you choose to ride this, please do it with respect for others as well as the trail itself.

Begin at the parking area for Switzer's Picnic Area, clearly signed along Angeles Crest Highway just east of the junction with Angeles Forest Highway. Switzer's Picnic Area is now closed to motorized traffic. You can find parking in the dirt lot on Angeles Crest Highway above the picnic area.

0.0 mile. From the parking area it is straightforward uphill pavement riding to Red Box. Angeles Crest Highway switchbacks around and steepens until it reaches Red Box at 4.8 miles. There are bathrooms and a drinking fountain at Red Box. Let the sweat dry and look around a bit. Interestingly enough, this place is named for a red box belonging to the fire department that is shown in early photos of the area and is still here today. Southeast and below you, the West Fork of the San Gabriel River begins its course to the huge drainage of the San Gabriel Canyon above Azusa. The Red Box/Rincon Road follows this path and starts from this parking lot (see Red Box/Rincon Road Loop in Chapter 4). The paved road to Mt. Wilson and San Gabriel Peak also starts here.

From the northwest corner of the parking lot, the Gabrielino Trail drops toward Switzer's. Take this trail and continue. Tight at first, the trail opens up to more of a road width every so often. The wide trail descends at a moderate grade through the pine and oak wooded canyon, then winds and twists its way to the canyon floor. Numerous rocks and stutter bumps in the corners will help keep you from daydreaming too much. At the junction at 7.1 miles, keep left and descend toward Switzer's Camp. The trail briefly gets rockier and more technical. At 7.2 miles, the stream comes into view on your right and begins to parallel the trail. As you cruise along, you catch glimpses of the creek with its numerous concrete waterfalls. If you're alert you will also catch glimpses (and hopefully glimpses only) of the plentiful trailside poison oak. Thus far you've been riding above the creek, but at 7.7 miles, two switchbacks bring you down to the water.

The trail now begins to roll, crisscrossing the cool waters, then climbing the banks and descending to the creek once again. Starting at 8.5 miles, small trailside plaques describe some of the native vegetation. You are approaching Switzer's picnic area now, so keep a tight hold on the reins; this is a heavily used area. Switzer's appears at 8.9 miles. Go right across the bridge and follow the pavement as it climbs a steep half mile back up to Angeles Crest Highway and your car.

Mt. Lowe/Echo Mountain Loop

Trip Length: 12.5 miles
Time Allowed: 3+ hours
Difficulty: Very strenuous, nontechnical to very technical
Elevation Gain: 2,800'
Ride Type: Loop, pavement, fire road, singletrack
Topo Map: Pasadena, Mt. Wilson
Comments: Highly recommended. There is a lot of history here, and a little knowledge about the Mt. Lowe Railway will add to the enjoyment. A quick look at the story of the "railway to the clouds" is included in the ride text, but to learn more, read Charles Seims' book, *Mount Lowe: The Railway in the Clouds.* The first 2.5 miles of steep pavement is by far the most difficult, and once you hit the dirt, the grade eases considerably. This ride can easily be broken up into shorter (and easier) rides, although no matter what, you need to make it past the brutal pavement section. For example, riding out to the ruins at Echo Mountain would be 3.5 miles one way and would be a possible, but strenuous, beginner ride.

Follow the trailhead directions for the Brown Mountain from Millard Campground ride until you reach the top of Chaney Trail at Sunset Ridge. Here the road splits to drop left into Millard Campground and head right up to Mt. Lowe. The road to Mt. Lowe is gated at this inter-section. Parking at this area is limited and fills up quickly on the week-ends. If it is full, you can start from the Millard Campground parking lot, although this would add a tough climb up from Millard to the gate at the Mt. Lowe Road.

0.0 mile. Begin at the gate. Even though it is paved, this first section of road up to the Cape of Good Hope is by far the most strenu-ous of the trip. Plug along, enjoying the view of the city below, and I'll tell you a story about a man and his vision.

In 1888, Professor Thaddeus Sobieski Coulincourt Lowe ("Thad" to his friends), Civil War balloonist extraordinaire and self-made man, settled in Pasadena with retirement in mind. Professor Lowe was no couch potato, however, and he felt like a man without a mission. Look-ing up into the San Gabriels every day from his home, Lowe was inspired to do something. He just didn't know what. In 1890, he had a fateful meeting with another visionary, David MacPherson, an engi-neer by trade. Together they hatched a plan to build a railway to the summit of Mt. Wilson, carrying folks up into the heights of the front country for a modest fee. Problems with easements dashed their hopes of ascending Mt. Wilson, so they turned their attention to a lesser peak, Echo Mountain. MacPherson oversaw the construction of a cog-wheel railway from Rubio Canyon up to Echo Mountain, a marvelous feat of engineering. The "Great Rubio Incline" exceeded a 60 percent grade in some places and rose some 1,300 feet in a little over half a mile. Real pixie ring stuff. At the end of the incline, Professor Lowe built a hotel, a small observatory, and a zoo. All this came to be known as the "White City." In 1893, the first public trip was conducted on the railway. To much fanfare, honored guests were winched up the incline by a 3,000-pound cable attached to a great bullwheel located on the mountaintop.

The Echo Mountain complex was a great success, and Professor Lowe set out to continue his railway up into the San Gabriels to the summit of Mt. Lowe. The railway never quite reached the top of Mt. Lowe, but it did follow a winding and scenic four-mile course up to Crystal Springs, a beautiful oak-shaded cove on the side of Mt. Lowe, where he constructed Ye Alpine Tavern, a Swiss chalet style resort. Scores of people rode the railway into the mountains and hiked, rode horses, played tennis, or just lounged around the tavern, enjoying the remote beauty of the forest. Although seemingly very successful, the endeavor placed a great financial strain on Lowe, and he lost his beloved railroad to mounting debts. Although operated by other parties into the twentieth century, an unsure economy and changed interests on the part of the public brought a gradual decline to the railway. Fire and other natural disasters spelled the end for Professor Lowe's dream, and by the late 1930s, the Mt. Lowe Railway had ceased operation.

Back to the ride! Still on the pavement, at 1.5 miles, stay right. At 1.7 miles you pass a gate and a sign that reads: *1.5 Miles—Echo Mountain 3.5 Miles—Mt. Lowe Campground 1.7 Miles—Mt. Wilson Road.* Just past here there's a roadside map showing the old railway route. A little more cranking brings you to the trailhead of the Sunset Ridge Trail (on the left). This nicely technical trail takes you back to the gate at Chaney Drive. Past Sunset Trail is the Echo Mountain Trail (on the right) to—surprise, surprise—Echo Mountain. Both of these trails will be ridden later in the ride on the return trip, but anyone who is too pooped to pedal uphill anymore would be well advised to ride out to Echo Mountain and explore the ruins of the White City before returning home. A little farther up the Mt. Lowe Road, the pavement ends at the Cape of Good Hope, and you begin to ride on the route of the original railway. This is a nice railroad grade and is much easier than the pavement behind you. As the miles pass by, you ride through history, passing such noted locations as the Circular Bridge (3.3 miles) where the railway negotiated a sharp curve by means of a trestle over

the canyon below, and the Granite Gate (4.4 miles) where the railway bed was blasted through solid rock. Some of the original electrical wires that supplied power to the railway cars are still visible here. At 5.2 miles and 1.5 hours, you reach the Mt. Lowe Campground, built on the site of the Alpine Tavern. This is a fine lunch spot; the climbing is mostly over and it's fun to sit on the ruins of the tavern and imagine what it was like here during the tavern's heyday some 90 years ago.

Back on the Mt. Lowe Road, ride a little bit farther uphill (0.3 mile) to an intersection with the road to Inspiration Point and the Idlehour and Sam Merrill trailheads. Mt. Wilson is plainly visible; the Mt. Lowe Road continues around San Gabriel Peak before intersecting with the road to Mt. Wilson and Red Box. Stop climbing here and take a quick little jaunt out to Inspiration Point before hitting the Sam Merrill Trail. To get to the point, take a right up the fire road and ride the short distance out to some ruins where sighting tubes point out distant landmarks like Venice, the Rose Bowl, Los Angeles, etc. But it is a rare, clear day that a peek through the pipes provides anything other than haze. Note: The Castle Canyon Trail that takes off from here is *not recommended* as a bike trail. Return to the trailhead for the Sam Merrill, on the left now at 6.0 miles, and turn left onto the single-track. This trail has many personalities in its 2.6 miles to Echo Mountain. It is attractive and shaded, then exposed and rocky, and mostly always technical and challenging. If exposure makes you nervous, this is not the trail for you. You would be better off backtracking down the fire road that you came up.

On one of the large rock outcroppings in the lower part of the trail, I suffered my first double pinch flat of the year, a dubious accomplishment indeed. There are also many sharp switchbacks to negotiate, and proper riding techniques are required to reduce the impact on the trail structures. Some are better walked than ridden. Don't brakeslide! As always, ride softly and watch for other trail users. At 8.6 miles you reach the ruins at Echo Mountain. As you intersect with the Echo Mountain Trail (to the right), the Sam Merrill continues on down the mountainside. NOT recommended for bikes, this section is very narrow, tight, and exposed. If you like, take a left and ride out to the ruins of the White City, past the great bullwheel and the ruins of the power house. There are still remnants of the railroad tracks heading toward the precipice into Rubio Canyon. To continue the ride, follow the Echo Mountain Trail back out to the pavement of the Cape of Good Hope, visible to the west. This short section of railroad bed makes a fine trail, although there is some exposure, so use caution. There are a lot of hikers using this and the Sunset Ridge Trail to come, so be good boys and girls.

Back on the pavement at 9.6 miles, turn left and ride 150 feet or so to the trailhead for the Sunset Ridge Trail. Turn right and proceed onto the trail. Still a technical trail (winding above Millard Canyon), it is more shaded and damp than the Sam Merrill. Watch for poison oak! It thrives here. As with the Sam Merrill, there are several tight switchbacks to negotiate. At 10.6 miles, you come to a paved spur road from the Mt. Lowe Road. Continue straight ahead on the trail. This last section of trail is mellow and rolling. At 11.6, stay left. At 12.1, you are back at the pavement of the Mt. Lowe Road, and a right turn brings you down to the gate and your starting point–12.5 miles and about 3 hours later.

If you had to park down in Millard Canyon, you can catch one more piece of singletrack. As you head down paved Mt. Lowe Road on your way to the gate, keep your eyes peeled for a last bit of the Sunset Trail on your right, across from the water tank. Cool and shady, this trail is generally easy with only a few tricky sections and a handful of switchbacks. It deposits you at Millard Campground, where you go left to your car in the parking area.

Idlehour Trail

Trip Length: 15 miles
Time Allowed: 4+ hours
Difficulty: Very strenuous, very technical
Elevation Gain: 3,000'
Ride Type: Loop (with or without car shuttle), fire road, trail
Road Number: 12W16
Topo Map: Pasadena, Mt. Wilson
Comments: Great trail! This is technically easier than the Sam Merrill and Sunset trails but not by much. It is much prettier though. If there hasn't been much recent trail work here, it can be very brushy—cheese grater time! Also expect some portaging in the creek bed.

Since Idlehour Trail is best done from Mt. Lowe to Mt. Wilson Toll Road, this leaves you with the option of a car shuttle to avoid the city street return back to Chaney Trail from Crescent Drive at Eaton Canyon. I elect to use a car shuttle, so my mileage does not reflect any mileage incurred on the return to the starting point.

To arrange a car shuttle, leave your return vehicle at the Mt. Wilson Toll Road trailhead (see following trail description). Take your other vehicle to the ride start at the Mt. Lowe Road gate at the top of Chaney Trail (see directions in the Brown Mountain from Millard Campground ride).

Follow the directions for the Mt. Lowe/Echo Mountain Loop and ride until you reach the split in the fire road (2N50) for Inspiration Point at 5.5 miles. The Sam Merrill Trail is to the right and Idlehour Trail is to the left. Turn onto the Idlehour Trail and prepare to enjoy yourself! This is a great trail, not too steep or narrow, just about perfect. There will be some sections that test your skills and nerve, but for the most part it's no real problem for an experienced mountain cyclist. Mind your velocity so as not to surprise any hikers or so a sharp turn doesn't surprise you! It doesn't take long to drop into the creek bottom at 7.5 miles where the trail crosses the creek and rises sharply up the opposite wall of the canyon. This is an incredibly beautiful spot, as is most of the ride to come.

Push and ride for a while until you top out on a small ridge, cross over its crest, and drop into the shaded canyon once again. From this ridge, Mt. Wilson looms above. The section of trail before you is a little more treacherous, narrow and rocky, but soon you are back at creek level. From here it is ride/carry, plonk along, etc., through the creek bottom. Trials lovers will enjoy this part. The rest of you. . . . well at least it is really pretty. It's this beauty that attracted Emil Gunther to Eaton Canyon in 1915, when he established Camp Idlehour in the canyon. The secluded resort catered to guests until its closing in 1932. The canyon is secluded and beautiful even now, but the resort is only fading ruins. Note: My mileage through this section of creek bed is somewhat suspect due to the amount of portaging and slow riding speeds involved.

At 9.3 miles, you reach Idlehour Trail Camp. On the right of the trail, just before you reach the campground proper, there is a lovely waterfall where the stream courses over a 10-foot boulder. The trail turns left out of the campground and soon begins an honest uphill pursuit of the Toll Road. This is steep and is a good workout whether you are riding or pushing, although I was able to ride nearly all of it. Eaton Canyon falls quickly away, and at 10.2 miles the grade eases and the trail actually turns downhill for a portion before it hooks up with the Toll Road at 11.1 miles—about 3 hours into the ride.

It's all downhill from here to the bottom of the Toll Road, so mind your speed. Note: There is a 15 mph speed limit on the Toll Road for a good reason. The Toll Road sees a lot of user-traffic, including equestrians and numerous youth groups, so slow down, be friendly and say hello to folks instead of blowing their doors off.

Directions to the bottom are as follows. From Idlehour Trail, turn right on the Toll Road. At 11.6 miles, turn left. At 12.1 miles, turn left. You are now riding through Henninger Flats, operated by Los Angeles County. Henninger Flats has camping by permit, as well as a small museum, water, restrooms, a lookout tower, and a log cabin display. Continue through the picnic area and down the Toll Road. At 15.5 miles, you hit the bottom of the Toll Road and cross the Eaton Canyon bridge. Climb up a steep little bit of pavement and pass through the gate to Crescent Drive. If you elected for a shuttle, your ride is over.

Mt. Wilson Toll Road

Trip Length: Varies. 5.5 to 18 miles
Time Allowed: 1 to 4 hours
Difficulty: Very long and strenuous, fairly technical due to steep grade on return
Elevation Gain: 4,500' maximum
Ride Type: Fire road out-and-back
Road Number: 2N45
Topo Map: Mt. Wilson
Comments: This is one of the classic Southern California mountain bike rides and is a benchmark for anyone wanting to test his or her fitness level against the consistently steep grade of the Toll Road. The large amount of variance in riding time and mileage takes into account that this is not an all-or-nothing ride. Many cyclists make Henninger Flats Campground their goal and leave the summit of Mt. Wilson to hardier folks. This is not the ride to do on a hot smoggy day.
Note: The amount of traffic that any weekend brings to the Toll Road has resulted in some incidents involving cyclists and equestrians. This is a heavily used pathway and demands the utmost in caution when you are coming back off the top. The prolonged, steep grade makes high speeds readily attainable, but there is a posted speed limit of 15 miles per hour on the Toll Road. Don't be a "bonehead on a bike." Save the heroic high-speed antics for some less-travelled backcountry route, or better yet, the race course.

The entrance to the Mt. Wilson Toll Road is off Pinecrest Drive in Altadena. The easiest way to get there from the 210 Freeway is to exit at Sierra Madre and turn left on Altadena Drive. Follow Altadena Drive to Crescent Drive. Turn right, then turn right again on Pinecrest Drive. There is an entrance on the right of the road at a gated chain-link fence that drops into Eaton Canyon and heads up the Toll Road. It is a little obscure to locate, but chances are you will see other folks milling about the entrance.

Homeowners here have complained about the parking situation

at the Toll Road. You might consider leaving your vehicle at Eaton Canyon Park or one of several dirt lots lining the canyon along Altadena Drive, then riding to the Toll Road entrance. This would help ease tensions considerably. If you do park at the Toll Road gate, please be quiet—especially early on weekend mornings—and be careful not to block driveways.

One final note: The Toll Road was the center of a major wildfire in the fall of 1993. You will see the effects of the fire as you make your way up to and through Henninger Flats. After the fire, the Toll Road was closed for many months while Forest Service work crews used the road to truck out debris. No sooner had the Toll Road been opened for recreational use than a huge landslide just above the Eaton Canyon bridge closed it again. At press time the Toll Road was open, but soil erosion continues to be a problem. Check with the Arroyo Seco Ranger District before riding in the area. (If you're planning a night ride, forget it; the gate at the entrance is locked at dusk.)

0.0 mile. Ride through the gate and drop down into Eaton Canyon, crossing the bridge, and begin to climb the Toll Road. Steep, isn't it? Get used to it. Learn to love it. There are 9 miles to go. You will quickly gain elevation and before long, Altadena will be far below. There are many turnouts where you can look around. Let's stop at one and talk about some of Mt. Wilson's history.

Mt. Wilson is named after Benjamin Wilson, owner of a local vineyard. He looked at Mt. Wilson as a source of lumber for fencing and wine barrels. Later, looking to exploit the mountain in a different way, a private enterprise built the first developed pathway to the top with the intent of charging for through-passage. In 1891, the Toll Road opened to the public as a trail with the "toll" being 25 cents for foot traffic and 50 cents for people on horseback. The Toll Road was a very popular, though rugged trip and many hardy souls found their way to the summit by way of it. As years went by, the trail was widened to accommodate vehicle traffic and the transport of a 60-inch telescope to the top of the mountain. Later, bigger and better observatories were designed and a bigger and better road was required to transport the equipment, resulting in the final road width of 10 feet. All the widening was done by hand! As you suffer along, think about that. Maybe it will make you feel better. All through this time, the Toll Road drew scores of people to Mt. Wilson. This was a grand time in the history of the mountain. A hotel was built on top and gracefully met the needs of weary travellers who arrived on foot, horseback, or in more com-

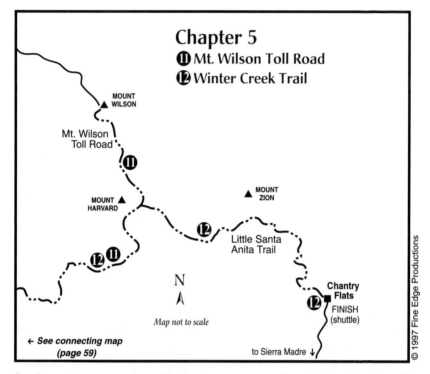

Chapter 5
⓫ Mt. Wilson Toll Road
⓬ Winter Creek Trail

MOUNT WILSON

Mt. Wilson Toll Road

MOUNT HARVARD

MOUNT ZION

Little Santa Anita Trail

N

Map not to scale

Chantry Flats

FINISH (shuttle)

← **See connecting map (page 59)**

to Sierra Madre ↓

© 1997 Fine Edge Productions

fort by private car or bus. The late 1920s saw a slow decline for the Toll Road, however. Angeles Crest Highway was pushing its way into the forest and, when it reached Red Box, soon gave the public an easy option to the top of Wilson. There was no way the Toll Road could compete with a modern, public highway, and it soon ceased operation and was turned over to the U.S. Forest Service. The hotel was torn down in 1966 to make way for Skyline Park.

Back to our ride. At 2.7 miles, you come to Henninger Flats Campground. Named for "Captain" William K. Henninger, a rancher-farmer in the area around 1880, Henninger Flats is a lovely campground and is the destination for many travellers on the Toll Road. There are water and restrooms here. Henninger Flats is operated by Los Angeles County, which allows camping by permit. There is also a display of a restored log cabin and lookout tower here. If you are feeling a little worse for wear, this is a good spot to turn back. To continue on, the Toll Road picks up again through the campground and to the right. At the road to the heliport, turn right and continue up. The worst part of the climbing is behind you, but the road is still pretty tough. Unlike the bottom 3 miles, the landscape along the upper section of the Toll

Road is at times well shaded and always quite lovely. At 3.4 miles you pass Idlehour Trail.

At 7.5 miles you pass the Little Santa Anita Trail, and just as you pass the trailhead, you can look up ahead to the communication towers on Mt. Wilson. Every TV station in Los Angeles and many radio stations broadcast from here, and the mountaintop fairly bristles with metal structures. A little more grinding brings you to the pavement at 9 miles. This is a steep little section of pavement that takes you to a small gate. With towers on the right and towers on the left, ride around the gate and onto level pavement. Turn right and ride through the gate to Skyline Park (park closed). Yes, you really did ride all the way up here, you animal you. The observatories are visible as bald-headed buildings in the distance.

The return trip down the Toll Road is potentially very fast and furious. Please use common sense and control your speed at all times. To return to your starting point at Eaton Canyon, simply retrace your route down the mountain.

Winter Creek Trail

Trip Length: 5.6 miles (trail only); 16.8 miles total ride
Time Allowed: 4+ hours
Difficulty: Very strenuous, very technical
Elevation Gain: Depends. 3,800' to 4,000' if done from bottom of Toll Road
Ride Type: Fire road and trail, best done as a shuttle
Road Numbers: 11W20, 11W23
Topo Map: Mt. Wilson
Comments: This is a very demanding and equally rewarding trail. Beginning at its high point off the Toll Road just below the summit of Mt. Wilson, the Winter Creek Trail is a *tour de force* of beauty and challenge to its end at Chantry Flat. This is probably best done as a shuttle with one vehicle at the bottom of the Toll Road and another at Chantry Flats. This eliminates the drudge on city streets back to your starting point.

Follow the parking and riding instructions in the Mt. Wilson Toll Road ride in this chapter until you reach the trailhead for the Little Santa Anita Trail on the right. You need not continue, but the top of Mt. Wilson is only 1.5 miles farther, and it seems a shame not to ride to the top after working so hard. I'll wait here while you continue to the top. Back already? Good. Riding to the top added 3.7 miles or so to your computer, so if you chose not to summit the mountain, subtract 3.7 miles from all further mileages.

The trail drops sharply into a rocky and difficult section and is a taste of the next section to come. For a while, the trail is rutted and sandy and will demand full concentration and smooth riding techniques to conquer. I walked some of the nastier sections to preserve both the surface of my body and the trail. This rugged section doesn't last long. At 11.2 miles, keep left. At 11.7 miles, a trail sign reads *Hoegee's Camp 2 miles, Sierra Madre 5 miles, Mt. Wilson 2 miles.* Go left and up, following the Winter Creek Trail. After a steep, technical section, you go quickly down a rolling, rutted section to 12.5 miles, where the trail bends sharply to the left and disappears into a stand of oak trees.

Prepare for a total change in character in the trail. Heavily shaded and narrow, the trail contours down the hillside. Lush with ferns (and poison oak), it is an absolutely eye-popping ride. Having spent a week this same summer in Crested Butte, Colorado, I was used to this type of riding but didn't expect to find it here in the mountains of Southern California. Don't let the beauty turn your head too often, because you need all your skills to negotiate the tricky switchbacks and root sections that punctuate the trail at regular intervals. At 14.1 miles you reach a split in the trail as you near the canyon bottom. There is a sign here. The left trail goes down to Hoegee's Camp and continues in the creek bed, difficult and rocky. The upper section of the Winter Creek Trail continues to the right and up. (As an aside, Hoegee's Camp was founded in 1908 by Arie Hoegee and family and was a complete little resort, offering food, tent housing, supplies, and riding stables. Operating under different owners into the 1950s, it met its end by fire in 1953.)

Back on the upper Winter Creek Trail, you need to do some work for a while as you climb your way out of Winter Creek. Head up into the sunshine and the chaparral of an exposed east slope where the trail is rocky and dry as it snakes down to Chantry Flats and Santa Anita Canyon. Soon, at 16.4 miles, you come to a fire road. Turn left and zip down to Chantry Flats, at 16.8 miles and—by my watch—3 hours, 30 minutes of riding.

CHAPTER 6

Mt. Gleason and Vicinity

Rising out of the northern section of the Tujunga, Mt. Gleason's broad shoulders hold nice stands of pine and offer fine roads for exploring. The higher elevation here, around 6,500 feet, brings cooler temperatures year-round, and during most winters, the slopes of Mt. Gleason are covered with snow. Road 3N17 from Mill Creek Summit allows easy auto access to the top of Mt. Gleason on pavement and lends itself well to cycling, although it involves two good climbs to get there. For families, driving the road to the summit of Mt. Gleason and exploring the area by bicycle would be a great adventure for everyone.

Indian Canyon Road

Trip Length: 5.1 miles to Santa Clara Divide Road
Time Allowed: 1.5+ hours
Difficulty: Strenuous
Elevation Gain: 2,200'
Ride Type: Fire road
Road Number: 4N37
Topo Map: Agua Dulce
Comments: Used more by four-wheel-drive vehicles than mountain bikes, Indian Canyon road climbs out of Soledad Canyon up to 3N17, the Santa Clara Divide Road. It is a pretty tough climb, but makes for a long and fast downhill. Once you hit the Santa Clara Divide Road, you can turn right and work your way toward Magic Mountain or turn left and head toward North Fork Station and the Mt. Gleason area. Either direction makes for a pretty difficult ride. North Fork Station is only 4 miles to the left (east) but the road climbs and drops several times along the way, so don't let the mileage fool you.

Although you can approach Indian Canyon Road from either direction on Soledad Canyon Road, we get there from Acton as in the Mt. Gleason loop ride. From the 14 Freeway, exit at Crown Valley Road

81

and turn right (south). Follow Crown Valley Road to Soledad Canyon Road and turn right. After 5.2 miles, you reach 4N37, marked by a sign on the right of Soledad Canyon Road. On the way up you pass a wild animal preserve. I remember stopping there as a youth and peering down into the valley from behind tall fences trying to catch a glimpse of some African beast while strange animals calls echoed around me.

0.0 mile. Leaving the jungle sounds behind, Indian Canyon Road (4N37) begins very steeply and then descends for a moment into a very pretty canyon where sycamores line the creek. Splash across a small stream and begin to climb again. It is a pretty consistent climb, so be prepared to work a little. As you near the top, you pass through the second break in the dry chaparral-covered hills. A shaded northern drainage holding lacy fir trees, oaks, and big leaf maples is the first cool spot on the climb since you left the creek bottom. Soon, at 5.1 miles, you are at the top at the Santa Clara Divide Road (3N17). South over Pacoima Canyon is Mendenhall Ridge.

From here at Indian Canyon Road and 3N17, you can travel the Santa Clara Divide Road in either direction. Neither way is particularly easy travel; it's paved in sections, but hilly. To the west, towers sprout up on Magic Mountain 2.8 miles away and mostly uphill. North Fork Station is 4.4 miles to the east, and 3N17 continues on past North Fork to Messenger Flats Campground and Mt. Gleason. Mt. Gleason would be about 9.6 miles farther and Messenger Flats about 8 miles.

If you continue on toward North Fork, the ride back is just as hard as the ride there. Keep that in mind. In any case, the ride back down Indian Canyon Road is fast and furious, and you should be pretty well hammered when you finish at Soledad Canyon Road.

Mt. Gleason from Acton

Trip Length: 25 miles
Time Allowed: 3+ hours
Difficulty: Very strenuous
Elevation Gain: 3,500'
Ride Type: Loop on fire road and pavement
Road Numbers: 4N32, 4N33, 3N17, 4N24
Topo Map: Acton, Condor Peak
Comments: You can approach Mt. Gleason and reach its summit from many directions. This tough loop is a favorite of many riders from the Acton and Agua Dulce areas and is a great ride. Riding time for fit riders is under 3 hours, but allow ample time to rest and enjoy the ride.

Take the 14 Freeway east and exit at the Crown Valley Road offramp. Turn right on Crown Valley and drive 1.5 miles to Soledad Canyon Road. Turn left and drive 1.5 miles to Aliso Canyon Road. Turn right. There's a sign on the right 2.4 miles along indicating the Angeles National Forest boundary. Park here at the start of 4N32, which takes off directly from this point.

0.0 mile. Road 4N32 rolls along the dusty foothills of Mt. Gleason, which is plainly visible to the south. Can't see it? Look higher. Yes, way up there. You'll be there in a while, but for now keep an eye out for large, noisy trucks hauling loads from a mining operation farther up 4N32. Most of the time you are travelling under high voltage lines, and the crackling of the electricity mixes with the whirring of your freewheel.

At 3.7 miles, turn left and pass the quarry. At 4.4 miles, you intersect with 4N33. The sign here reads: *Soledad Turnoff 2 Miles, Aliso Canyon Road 5 Miles, North Fork Station 7 Miles.* Go left on 4N33 and begin a long climb up Moody Canyon—sure to get your blood pumping. More rocky than steep, the first 2 miles or so of 4N33 are some of the most difficult. At 6.1 miles, on the outside of a left-hand sweeper overlooking Acton, Vasquez Rocks County Park, and the Sierra Pelona, is a stone marker announcing Perspiration Point. Honoring the CCC workers of the depression years, the marker—missing the pick and shovel that used to adorn it—shows the ravages of time and vandals.

At 8 miles, the vegetation changes, and you ride along a north-facing slope dotted with pines and scattered with cones. This is a short respite as you quickly move back into the typical chaparral of the lower elevations. It is, however, a hint of things to come. Looking ahead you can see stands of pine and cedar, and at 10 miles, 4N32 intersects with 3N17. The right path leads to North Fork Ranger Station and Magic Mountain. You turn left and continue climbing. At 10.9 miles, keep right. The left road climbs up to an electronic site.

At this point, the easy grade of the road makes for sweat-free views of Iron Mountain and Mendenhall Ridge to the south. Mile 11.4 brings you to Messenger Flats Campground. This is a beautiful spot to rest if you need to. (There are toilets here but they may be closed.) To

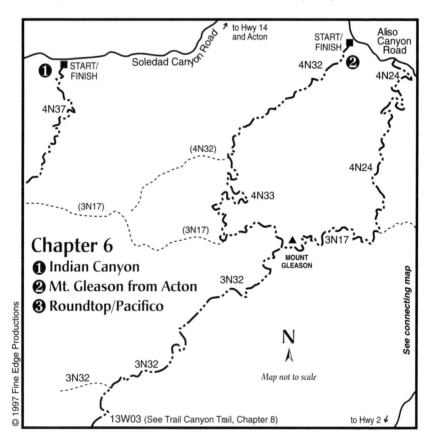

Chapter 6

❶ Indian Canyon
❷ Mt. Gleason from Acton
❸ Roundtop/Pacifico

© 1997 Fine Edge Productions

continue, rejoin 3N17 for the short climb up to Mt. Gleason. At 12.4 miles, you come to an intersection with 3N32, the road to Lightning Point Campground. Turn left and grind up the steep, paved road towards Gleason. Mile 12.7 finds you at the top of the hill. To get to the actual top of Mt. Gleason, turn left past the gate and ride just a little bit farther. Note: This mileage is not accounted for.

If you didn't stop at Messenger Flats, try this area for a nice rest. The remainder of the ride is easy compared to what you left behind, so this is a good lunch spot. After all, you've gained over 3,000 feet of elevation and could probably use a Twinkie or two. To continue, rejoin 3N17, still paved at this point, and drop off the face of the earth. Just kidding, but it is a very rapid descent down a windy, paved road. The corners sneak up on you, and motor vehicle traffic is common. Be careful! At 14.8 miles, the pavement turns to dirt, climbing a little, then popping out on the pavement again at 15.3 miles. On your left is State Correctional Facility #16 (i.e. prison camp). Stay out unless you intend to move in for a while.

Turn right onto the pavement and cruise along to 15.8 miles, at which point you turn left onto a dirt road, 4N24. A little way down 4N24, Pacific Crest Trail crosses. It is unsigned and tempting to ride, but closed to bicycle travel. Now you climb and descend, but mainly descend as you start into a truly great downhill that seems to last forever. You keep Gleason Canyon on your left and Bear Trap Canyon on your right.

to Hwy 14

Aliso Canyon Rd.

N3

PACIFICO MOUNTAIN

START/ FINISH

3

3N17

GRANITE MOUNTAIN

3N90

Angeles Forest Highway

ROUNDTOP

N3

See connecting map

© 1997 Fine Edge Productions

■ Ride Start/Finish
▪▪▪ Mountain Bike Route
━━ Paved Road
▬▬ Freeway
▪▪▪▪ Other Roads and Trails
(bikes may be off limits)

In 1889, a large grizzly bear named "Monarch" was terrorizing the surrounding ranches. Finally located in this canyon and trapped by a "bear posse," he was taken to the San Francisco Zoo. You don't have to worry about grizzlies these days, but there are several places to make a wrong turn and some of the roads do not appear on any map. Pay attention.

Bear left at 16.0 miles and 16.2 miles. At 18.2, 19.3, and 21.8 miles, stay right. You are almost on the valley floor now and have been keeping Aliso Canyon Road over your right shoulder as you dropped down towards it. A short, steep climb and a right turn at 22.8 miles takes you under some high voltage towers and brings you quickly down to Aliso Canyon Road. Turn left on the pavement (23.2 miles to this point) and continue an easy cruise to your starting point 24.4 miles ago.

Roundtop/Pacifico

Trip Length: 19 miles
Time Allowed: 2 hours, 30 minutes
Difficulty: Very strenuous, technical if you take the four-wheel-drive loop option
Elevation Gain: 2,400'
Ride Type: In-and-out, fire road
Road Number: 3N17
Topo Map: Pacifico Mountain, Chilao Flats
Comments: A sister mountain to Mt. Gleason, Mt. Pacifico is 7,000 feet high and just as lovely. Crisscrossed with jeep roads to explore, it hosts a very nice campground, Pacifico Campground. You reach the summit by way of a long and constant climb. This ride also visits Roundtop and Granite mountains, although they are off a side road and are optional.

The ride begins at Mill Creek Summit Rest Area, located on Angeles Forest Highway. It can be reached via Angeles Forest Highway from Highway 14, or from the 210 to Angeles Crest Highway and Angeles Forest Highway. Both ways are well signed. At the rest area, 3N17 descends from the east face of Mt. Gleason and crosses Angeles Forest Highway before heading up toward Mt. Pacifico. Mill Creek Rest Area has toilets in case you want to start in comfort. You may start from here or drive up 3N17 through Mill Creek Station and park at the end of the pavement at the parking lot where there are restroom facilities and good water. The parking lot is for day-use only, and the gate at Angeles Crest Highway may close at dusk. If you plan to take a long time on your trip, it would be best to check this out or park at the rest area at the highway.

Starting from the upper parking area, 0.0 mile, go up 3N17, past the gate and onto the dirt. This isn't a really difficult climb, but it is constant and gives you little rest. One of the nicest things about riding the north side of the range at these higher elevations is the nifty view into the Antelope Valley and on rare, clear days, to the Tehachapis and beyond. The patchwork of the valley floor is quite a sight. At 3.2 miles, you reach the intersection with the road to Roundtop Mountain. The trip out to Roundtop and back is a worthwhile diversion if you're not too tuckered out, and offers a different perspective of the Pacifico area. As you are standing there at the crossroads munching your Power Bar and deciding which way to go, there is a time-worn and decrepit trail that takes off to the left of the sign that points the way to Mt. Pacifico. This "trail" skirts the north side of the mountain and is not rideable, but a short, careful scramble out a ways offers you an outstanding look down Tie Canyon towards Aliso Canyon Road.

Feeling up to the challenge of a little side trip? Good. Then Roundtop it is. Turn right on 3N90 where a sign reads *Granite Mountain—1 Mile, Roundtop Mountain—3 Miles.* (The campground on Roundtop no longer exists.) This is a rollercoaster of a road and a good workout up to the end 6.2 miles later on the 6,300-foot-high Roundtop Mountain. From here, you have a clear view over Chilao Flats and Angeles Crest Highway into the San Gabriel Wilderness.

Between you and Chilao Flats, located in Alder Creek, is the Loomis Ranch. In 1913, Captain Lester G. Loomis, his wife Grace, and their three daughters established a ranch at the old Tom Clark Cabin site. They also built an arrastre and did a little gold mining. The Loomis hospitality became well known, and hikers and hunters heading to Chilao and Buckhorn always found a welcome bed and a good meal. To capitalize on this, Captain Loomis began to charge 50 cents each for a meal and a bed, and his ranch developed into a very successful enterprise. The decrease of people on foot in the backcountry started a decline of the Loomis Ranch, and in 1936, Captain Loomis died. The ranch property changed hands several times, but is still privately held. The 50 cent meals are gone, as is the era of the trailside camp and resort.

There is no place to go but back the way you came to 3N17. A right turn towards Mt. Pacifico continues the ride. At 9.1 miles, continue past a small, steep four-wheel-drive road. A return option that uses this road will be discussed later. At 10.3 miles, turn left and head up. At 11.4 miles you pop out on top of Mt. Pacifico.

There are a myriad of paths to explore, but if you keep left and continue climbing a little more, you will reach Pacifico Campground at 11.9 miles. Situated amidst boulders large and small, and well shaded by large pines, this is a beautiful campground where you can have lunch and scramble around on granite rocks. There are tables and pit toilets. Looking down towards the desert floor, Little Rock Reservoir is the small blue puddle 4,000 feet below. When you tire of clear, thin air and solitude (if you ever do), returning to your vehicle is a downhill joy as you retrace your path down the mountain.

If you're looking for a more adventurous and technically challenging route off Mt. Pacifico, the four-wheel-drive road you passed on your way up at 9.1 miles will do nicely. Ride down the main road off the mountain, until at 13.1 miles (about 1 mile from the campground), you can take a branch road off to the right. You know you are on the right road when you see the Pacific Crest Trail crossing nearby. (The Pacific Crest Trail is closed to bicycle traffic.) Follow the four-wheel-drive road up steep, challenging climbs and nasty downhills. At 13.7 miles turn left, then right again and continue west along the ridge. At 14.2 miles, you pop up on a small hill and can see down to Mill Creek Summit. From here it gets somewhat confusing, since there are numerous paths to choose from. You can see 3N17 below you to your left, though, and with a little searching, the path down to it is obvious. It is also rough, rocky and knee deep in whoop-dees. When you drop onto 3N17, turn right and enjoy a really nice and rapid cruise back to your car at Mill Creek Summit. At 18.6 miles, you are there!

CHAPTER 7

The Verdugo Mountains

Some of the best rides are epic journeys that require hours of time to complete and cover vast and difficult distances into the backcountry of a mountain region. However, the realities of modern life often conspire to make these long rides few and far between. Often, the typical mountain bike ride is fit it into a busy schedule, after work or early morning, and lasts two hours or less. If you're lucky, your ride can take place within a short distance of the urban area in which you live. The Verdugo Mountains fill this bill very nicely, thank you. Situated northeast of the busy cities of Glendale and Burbank, and close to Pasadena, the Verdugos offer easy access from both the I-5 and 210 Freeways.

Riding in the Verdugos is tailor-made for the after-work or Sunday morning cyclist. Moderate grades on good fire roads climb past dense chaparral and take you to nice viewpoints that look into the valley below and beyond the Los Angeles Basin. As they say, "all roads lead to Rome," and short climbs, typically 2 to 4 miles here, all lead to

the highest peak in the area, Verdugo Peak at 3,126 feet. The rides in this area are generally 10 miles or so in length, and to do 20 miles takes some imagination, but it's possible. You can find great riding spring through winter here; summer too, if you ride early enough in the day to avoid the typically poor air quality of the season. The Verdugo Mountains are jointly owned and administered by the City of Glendale and the Mountain Recreation and Conservation Authority. As of this writing, all the rides described here are open. Check with local authorities for updated information.

La Tuna Canyon Loop

Trip Length: 9.5 miles
Time Allowed: 90 minutes
Difficulty: Strenuous, technical
Elevation Gain: 1,600'
Ride Type: Loop, pavement, fire road, trail
Topo Map: Burbank
Comments: This loop uses a technical and difficult singletrack for its return and has a little of everything: climbing, downhill fire road, tricky and strenuous trail riding, and a pavement finish that begs for a last minute sprint against your riding buddies. Watch for poison oak on the singletrack.

Take the La Tuna Canyon offramp from the 210 Freeway onto La Tuna Canyon Road. Directly across the street from the bottom of the offramp is a gated paved road with some parking area at the gate; begin here. Chances are you will not be alone–this is a popular spot for runners, hikers, and cyclists to access the Verdugos.

0.0 mile at the gate. Follow the wide pavement east for 0.4 mile until the road splits. Turn right. Ride up a short but very steep paved road to where it turns to dirt and the grade lessens considerably. If you look around this point, you have some good views of the front range of the San Gabriels, and Mt. Lukens in particular. The rest of the fire road, now the Hostetter Fire Road, is not too tough and is middle chain ring if you feel ornery. At 3.4 miles, you intersect with the Verdugo Fire Road. There is a steel guard rail directly in front of you as you come to this point. I appreciate this, because sometimes I climb this hill so-o-o-o fast that I have trouble stopping at the top. Sure. Anyway, this is a nice viewpoint. Turn right and start on a fun downhill toward the La Tuna Canyon Trail.

At 4.2 miles keep right. Down, down, down you go to 5.8 miles where, on a promontory to the right, the trail starts its descent into a steep and narrow canyon. The trailhead is unsigned. If you reach the Stough Canyon Fire Road, you went too far by a half mile or so. The trail is easy to follow and runs the gamut of conditions from easy to "holy cow!" throughout its length. Keep an eye out for several old trucks off the side of the trail that have made this their final "rusting" place. You may think that all the climbing is over once you hit the trail. Wrong. The trail climbs a pretty good piece out of one canyon into another before finally ending at La Tuna Canyon Road at 8.2 miles. The last section of trail has two tricky switchbacks to negotiate before you hit the creek bottom. Once you are in the creek bed, keep to the right trail and climb sharply up to the road. You are now at La Tuna Canyon Road. A right turn on the pavement and 1.3 miles of pedaling takes you back to your starting point. Watch for fast traffic on La Tuna Canyon Road and keep an eye on the roadway; the lane narrows suddenly and you can find yourself riding in the traffic lane.

Brand Park Loop

Trip Length: 13 miles
Time Allowed: 2 hours
Difficulty: Strenuous, nontechnical
Elevation Gain: 2,000'
Ride Type: Loop, fire road, pavement
Topo Map: Burbank
Comments: This is a great loop and a good workout. The ride ascends Brand Fire Road, a steep and difficult climb, and then descends Stough Fire Road, adding a nice downhill off Verdugo Peak. The return is by way of Mountain Street and Sunset Canyon Drive.

To reach Brand Park, take I-5 to Magnolia Boulevard. Go north to North Sunset Canyon Drive and turn right. This becomes Mountain Street. Brand Park is on the north side of the street at Grandview Avenue. The fire road begins at the top left part of the park near the Doctor's House, a charming, restored house from a more gracious time in the city's past.

0.0 mile. Turn left at the white gate under the Doctor's House sign and head right. A steep paved road passes a debris basin and leads up to a gate at 0.2 mile. Pass by the gate and continue climbing. You pass through a small landfill on your way to Brand Fire Road, so obey the one-way signs and continue the very steep climb up the pavement. The pavement gives way to dirt and soon the road passes some crumbling foundations before turning right and leading into a pretty, shaded canyon. At 1 mile, in a sycamore shaded glen, the Brand lateral road splits from the main road. Go left and stay on the main road. Now, find those low gears and begin to claw your way toward the Verdugo Fire Road. This is a grunt but doesn't last long. At 3.7

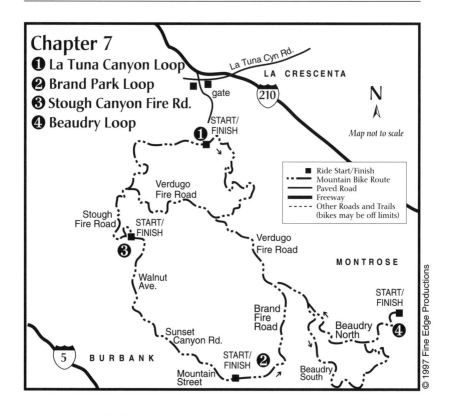

Chapter 7
❶ La Tuna Canyon Loop
❷ Brand Park Loop
❸ Stough Canyon Fire Rd.
❹ Beaudry Loop

La Tuna Cyn Rd.

LA CRESCENTA

gate

210

START/FINISH ❶

N

Map not to scale

■ Ride Start/Finish
∎ ∎ ∎ Mountain Bike Route
▬▬▬ Paved Road
▬▬▬ Freeway
- - - - Other Roads and Trails
(bikes may be off limits)

Verdugo Fire Road

Stough Fire Road

START/FINISH ❸

Verdugo Fire Road

MONTROSE

Walnut Ave.

START/FINISH ❹

Brand Fire Road

Beaudry North

Sunset Canyon Rd.

5 BURBANK

START/FINISH ❷

Mountain Street

Beaudry South

© 1997 Fine Edge Productions

miles, you reach the Verdugo Fire Road and, of all things, a bus bench, nicely placed to rest burning quads and look back over the city. Continuing on, ride left and up some more as you head toward Verdugo Peak and the radio towers perched atop the high points. At 4 miles, keep right. At 5.1 miles, keep left where Whiting Woods Fire Road comes up from Whiting Woods Road. At 5.5 miles or so, you top out and pass the electronic sites before dropping down to the Hostetter Fire Road from La Tuna Canyon at 5.8 miles. Keep straight ahead and begin a nearly uninterrupted descent down to Stough Canyon.

At 6.6 miles, keep right as you zip through a small pine plantation. At 7.7 miles, still dropping fast, the road affords a clear view to the south and west over the city below. At 8.2 miles, the La Tuna Canyon Trail drops to the right (see La Tuna Canyon Loop). At 8.7 miles, stay left on the Stough Canyon Fire Road. At 9.2 miles, stay left again. Then a short, steep section and a tight right turn drops you into the bottom of Stough Canyon. Continue past the debris basin and onto the pavement and the gate that blocks the road. Pass by the gate at 10 miles and drop down Walnut Avenue on a really fast paved descent. Watch for cars and golf carts from the nearby park and golf course. Follow Walnut Avenue down to Sunset Canyon Drive and turn left. The pavement return is almost as pleasant as the fire road, scenic and shaded with lovely homes and gently rolling big-ring climbs. Sunset Canyon Drive becomes Mountain Street, and at 12.9 miles you return to Brand Park and the start of your ride. Bring a picnic lunch and enjoy the park!

Stough Canyon Fire Road

Trip Length: 9 miles
Time Allowed: 90 minutes
Difficulty: Fairly strenuous, nontechnical
Elevation Gain: 1,600'
Ride Type: Out-and-back on fire road
Topo Map: Burbank
Comments: This is an easier climb than Brand Fire Road and eventually gets you to the same point at the top of the mountain. If you ride in the evening, you have excellent views of the city below.

From I-5, take Magnolia Boulevard and turn left onto Sunset Canyon Drive. Proceed to Walnut Avenue and turn right. Begin at the north end of Walnut Avenue along De Bell Golf Course. Past Stough Park, Walnut Avenue ends at a gate and the fire road picks up from here.

0.0 mile. Pass by the gate and continue a short distance on pavement until the dirt road begins, drops a little, then turns steeply to the left and begins the most difficult part of the entire climb in the first mile. Ugh! Grind along to 0.8 mile, at which point you keep right. At 1.3 miles, you intersect with the Verdugo Fire Road. The grade is quite a bit easier now, although it is all uphill for the next 4 miles. Turn right at 1.3 miles and head toward Verdugo Peak. At 2.3 miles, you roll onto a nice flat spot and come to an excellent viewpoint of the city below, of the Santa Monica Mountains, and if conditions allow, of the Pacific coastline. This is an especially nice spot late in the day when city lights shimmer in the cooling air. Continuing on, at 3.4 miles, keep left. A small pine tree plantation adds a foresty feeling to the otherwise chaparral-covered slopes as you near the top of the range.

The road rolls along with short, easy climbs and reaches the intersection with Hostetter Fire Road from La Tuna Canyon at 4.2 miles. This is another viewpoint over the city. Straight ahead and up Verdugo Fire Road you top out at 4.5 miles or so. Anywhere along here is a good place to stop, since you lose elevation rapidly if you continue. The return, back the way you came in, is a great downhill run, not too steep, but fast enough to keep you paying attention. Although this isn't used by hikers as much as Brand Fire Road is, please watch out for other folks on the way down. This is fun, but it isn't a race course. At 9 miles or so, you are back at Walnut Avenue.

Beaudry Loop

Trip Length: 11 miles
Time Allowed: 90+ minutes
Difficulty: Very strenuous, nontechnical
Elevation Gain: 1,800'
Ride Type: Fire road loop
Topo Map: Burbank, Pasadena
Comments: This is a fun loop in the east end of the Verdugos and is a good little workout. It is easier to ride up Beaudry North and descend Beaudry South because Beaudry South is steeper. However, if you have yet to meet the uphill you didn't like, try reversing the route and ride up the south road.

The entrance to Beaudry Fire Road is a little obscure. From the 210 Freeway exit at Pennsylvania Avenue, and turn right on Pennsylvania Avenue, which soon turns into Honolulu Avenue. Follow this to La Crescenta Avenue and turn right. In a few blocks, Oakmont View Drive turns to the right. Take this and then bear left onto Country Club Drive. Stay on Country Club Drive until you reach Beaudry Boulevard. Turn right. From the south parts of the valley, Canada Boulevard will take you to Country Club Drive and Beaudry Boulevard. The entrance to Beaudry Fire Road is located at 1300 Beaudry Boulevard at the point where Beaudry Boulevard becomes Beaudry Terrace.

0.0 mile. The entrance is a paved road lined with small sycamore trees. The road passes by a debris basin before meeting a gate on the fire road. Through the gate, the road heads up the canyon floor and begins to weave its way up into the mountains. At 0.4 mile you come to a split in the road where Beaudry North and South connect. The right path is the Beaudry North Road. Stay right and continue. At 2.5 miles, after a pretty tough climb, Beaudry South connects back in on the left and slightly behind you. If you want an awfully quick return trip, you may turn here to descend. Otherwise, continue to the top, an easier task than the last few miles. Keep right. At 3.1 miles you come to an intersection with Brand Fire Road. A bus bench here makes a handy resting spot, poised as it is overlooking Glendale. The top is just a little farther, so load up and move out.

From the bench, keep right and then right again at 3.4 miles, then left at 4.5 miles where Whiting Fire Road intersects on the left. From here to 5.0 miles or so, you are pretty much at the top and are riding in the shadows of microwave towers. At 5.0 miles, the road is paved and gravelly for a short time, then soon dives to the right and heads toward Hostetter Fire Road coming in from La Tuna Canyon. I avoided dropping down to this intersection so I wouldn't have any more uphill. Besides, the little promontory at the bend in the road at 5.0 miles is a nice "munchies" spot.

To return, retrace your path to Beaudry South at 7.5 miles and turn right, heading up rough pavement. Roll along for a while until the road begins to drop in earnest. This is a rollicking rollercoaster section, fast enough to make you pay attention. Watch for oncoming traffic. At 8.5 miles, stay left. The fire road on the right is the Verdugo Fire Road. After a nifty section of big whoop-dees, you reach the intersection of Beaudry North at 10.4 miles. Turn right and head back to the gate and Beaudry Boulevard.

CHAPTER 8

The Tujunga

The Tujunga District encompasses the westernmost section of the San Gabriel Mountains and is the largest of its four districts. The Tujunga generally consists of lower elevation chaparral-covered slopes and rounded, broad mountains. Hot in the summer, the Tujunga offers fine riding from autumn through spring and is generally accessible when the higher elevations of Angeles National Forest are snowbound. The one exception to this rule is the Mt. Gleason area of the Tujunga (see Chapter 6). Sitting at the headwaters of the massive Tujunga drainage, Mt. Gleason's 6,500-foot elevation practically guarantees yearly snowfall. That snow runoff and miles of other drainages from Pacifico to Charlton Flats wind their way to the Tujunga and collect here, rushing down to the cities of Sunland and Tujunga. Subject to periodic flooding, the Tujunga was dammed in 1931. In 1938, however, even this dam was not enough to hold back torrents of water that a great rainstorm dumped into the San Gabriels. The flood overran the dam and washed away the canyon below.

As you ride through here in drought years, it is difficult to imagine such flooding. Water is not easily found in this part of the National Forest, so carry plenty with you.

The Tujunga is bordered on the west by Sylmar and Freeways 210 and 14, on the north by Acton and the Soledad District, on the south by Sunland/Tujunga, and finally ending just east of Angeles Forest Highway. Road 3N17, the Santa Clara Divide Road, nearly bisects the entire district from its west end in Newhall to its eastern end at Angeles Crest Highway, near Chilao Flats. Although this book does not give a description to do so, it would be a long and demanding ride to complete this vast stretch of road in one journey. Still, it is tempting!

Wilson Canyon

Trip Length: 9 miles
Difficulty: Strenuous, nontechnical
Time Allowed: One hour approximately
Elevation Gain: 1,400'
Ride Type: Fire road out-and-back
Road Number: 3N56
Topo Map: San Fernando
Comments: This sandy, relatively steep climb gets easier as you near the top and is a nice evening ride! Starting behind Olive View Hospital, you can reach 3N56 by an equestrian path. The lower parts of this route are heavily used by our hooved friends, so ride appropriately.

Olive View Hospital is located north of the 210 Freeway, off Olive View Drive in Sylmar. Nearly destroyed by the Sylmar earthquake of 1971, what you see now of the hospital is largely rebuilt from the ruins. Oldtimers tell me that the valley floor below the hospital used to be covered with large olive orchards, hence the name.

To find the ride's starting point, turn at the emergency entrance to the hospital off Olive View Drive and drive straight back to a now unused pay-to-park lot. Beware of auto tire-killing spikes that ensure that you enter the appropriate driveway. Start at the trail to the east of the parking lot, adjacent to a flood control channel, which takes you to 3N56.

At several places on the sandy path, poles have been placed across the trail to prevent motorcycles from entering. Lift your bike over these poles; they are crank-high and will not bend, but you will. Labor along the sandy, twisty route under shady eucalyptus trees until you come to a fork in the trail at 0.1 mile. Turn left and head uphill. At 0.3 mile, you come to a short downhill, then a steep climb and a log crossing up to 3N56. Turn right. At 0.7 mile a stone pillar at the left has the road number inscribed on it. At 1.4 miles, keep right at the fork. Now there's nothing to do but stay on 3N56 and climb. Below and behind you, Sylmar and lower suburbia sprawl out. This makes a nice evening ride when you can admire the city lights twinkling in the fading twilight.

As you continue, the ride get a little easier—less sandy and not so steep. At 4.5 miles, you come to Wilson Canyon saddle where 3N56 meets 3N17 from Bear Divide/Camp Nine. (For more details, see the Camp Nine ride below.)

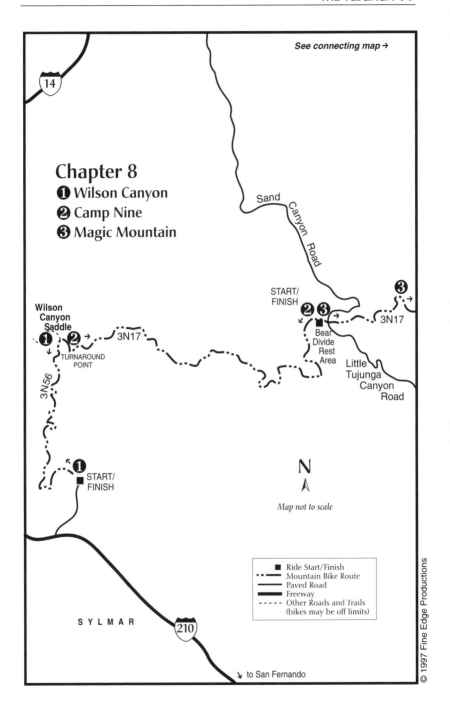

See connecting map →

Chapter 8

❶ Wilson Canyon
❷ Camp Nine
❸ Magic Mountain

Sand Canyon Road

Wilson Canyon Saddle

START/
FINISH

❶ ❷ → 3N17

TURNAROUND
POINT

3N56

❷ ❸
Bear
Divide
Rest
Area

❸
→
3N17

Little
Tujunga
Canyon
Road

❶ START/
FINISH

N

Map not to scale

■ Ride Start/Finish
▪-▪-▪ Mountain Bike Route
—— Paved Road
■■■ Freeway
- - - - Other Roads and Trails
(bikes may be off limits)

SYLMAR ⓿210

↘ to San Fernando

© 1997 Fine Edge Productions

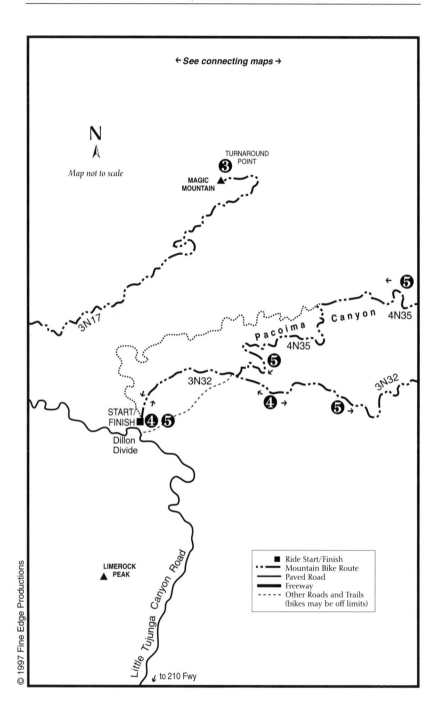

← *See connecting maps* →

N

Map not to scale

TURNAROUND POINT

MAGIC MOUNTAIN

❸

❺

3N17

P a c o i m a   C a n y o n

4N35

4N35

❺

3N32

3N32

❹

❺

START/ FINISH

❹ ❺

Dillon Divide

LIMEROCK PEAK

Little Tujunga Canyon Road

↓ to 210 Fwy

■ Ride Start/Finish
▪▪▪ Mountain Bike Route
── Paved Road
▬▬ Freeway
--- Other Roads and Trails
     (bikes may be off limits)

© 1997 Fine Edge Productions

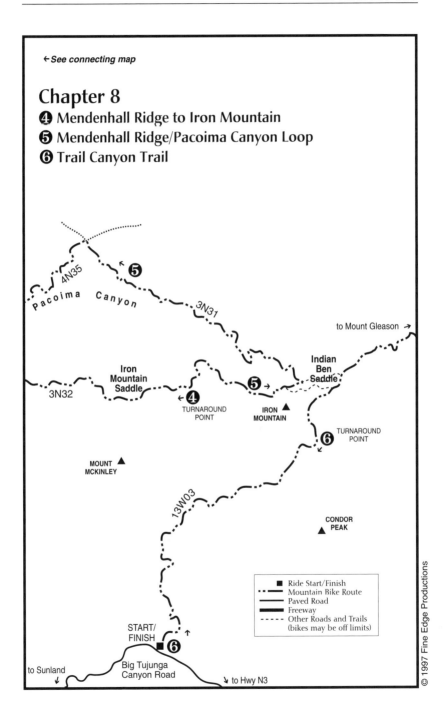

← *See connecting map*

Chapter 8
❹ Mendenhall Ridge to Iron Mountain
❺ Mendenhall Ridge/Pacoima Canyon Loop
❻ Trail Canyon Trail

4N35

Pacoima Canyon

3N31

to Mount Gleason →

Iron
Mountain
Saddle

3N32

Indian
Ben
Saddle

❺ →

❹ ←
TURNAROUND
POINT

IRON ▲
MOUNTAIN

❻
TURNAROUND
POINT

MOUNT ▲
MCKINLEY

13W03

CONDOR
▲ PEAK

■ Ride Start/Finish
∙∙∙∙∙ Mountain Bike Route
—— Paved Road
▬▬ Freeway
- - - Other Roads and Trails
        (bikes may be off limits)

START/
FINISH
■ ❻

to Sunland ↓

Big Tujunga
Canyon Road

↓ to Hwy N3

© 1997 Fine Edge Productions

There is nearly always a breeze at this pretty spot under the oaks. In the evening, carry a windbreaker to ward off the chill. The trip back down 3N56 is a great downhill. Have fun, but watch for equestrians, especially as you near the bottom.

Camp Nine

Trip Length: 8 to 20 miles
Time Allowed: From 1 to 2 hours
Difficulty: Fairly strenuous to strenuous
Elevation Gain: 1,200' to 2,000'
Ride Type: Out-and-back on pavement and fire road
Road Number: 3N17 west of Bear Divide
Topo Map: San Fernando
Comments: This route takes you past several nifty viewpoints of the San Fernando and Santa Clarita valleys. The overlooks have made this a popular midnight rendezvous spot. Los Angeles County Fire Camp Nine is accessed from this road, so watch for vehicle traffic.

To reach the trailhead, take Highway 14 to Sand Canyon Road and go south. Follow Sand Canyon to Bear Divide and the Bear Divide Rest Area (parking). From the San Gabriel Valley, take the Osborne exit off the 210. Go right and make the first left onto Osborne. Osborne becomes Little Tujunga Road as you continue to Bear Divide and parking at the rest area.

From the parking area, 3N17 heads west and climbs up a pretty stiff grade on a good paved road. On the left at 1.2 miles is a little promontory where you can catch your breath and look around. The mile or so you've travelled opens new vistas, and looking to the southeast you get a good view of six major peaks in the San Gabriels. Mt. Lukens, the peak farthest to the west, bristles with antennas. Mt. Wilson, in the background, is similarly adorned. More to the east you can see the broad, pine-covered top of Mt. Gleason. Below you, Little Tujunga Canyon Road winds toward Dillon Divide. Returning to 3N17, a little more pedaling takes you to another lookout spot. This time a more defined road leads off to the left and ends at a microwave site. Below you, set in a rugged canyon, Pacoima Reservoir looks poised and ready to spill into Sylmar.

Back on the road now and continuing up, up, up, at 4.2 miles you come to Los Angeles County Fire Camp Nine. This is a good turnaround point if you're tired. Continuing ahead tilts you the other way and you need to work your way back up 800 feet to return to this point. Still feeling fresh, you say? Read on.

Road 3N17 continues on through the compound past the heliport and comes to a fork at 4.9 miles. Take the right road and begin a nice downhill that takes you to the junction with 3N54, your computer showing 6.0 miles. Stay right and enjoy a fun, fast, downhill run to Wilson Canyon saddle and the junction with 3N56. (See the Wilson Canyon ride earlier in this chapter for more information.) From here, your possibilities narrow. Road 3N17 continues west, and an offshoot takes you up to some radio towers overlooking the east end of the Santa Clarita Valley. (3N17 continues down to San Fernando Road in Newhall, but runs into a locked gate at private property. *Do not continue down this road.*) Note: Trail 15W02, the Los Pinetos Trail, takes off from 3N17 near Wilson Saddle, but is closed to mountain bikes in the lower section where it enters Walker Ranch State Park.

Return to your starting point by way of 3N17, the reverse of your outward journey.

Magic Mountain

Trip Length: 13 miles
Difficulty: Fairly strenuous, but nontechnical
Time Allowed: 2 hours
Elevation Gain: 2,200'
Ride Type: out-and-back on paved road
Road Number: 3N17
Topo Map: San Fernando, Sunland, Agua Dulce
Comments: Road 3N17 from Sand Canyon Road to Magic Mountain is paved and in good condition. The long climb rewards you nicely with excellent views in all directions. Expect occasional vehicle traffic.

The easiest place to begin this ride is Bear Divide Rest Area (see directions for the Camp Nine ride above). Just 0.1 mile northeast of Bear Divide, back toward Sand Canyon, 3N17 (Santa Clara Divide Road) branches off from Sand Canyon Road and heads east toward Magic Mountain and points beyond. As Forest Service roads go, 3N17 is a major artery. A peek at the Angeles National Forest map shows it continuing to Angeles Crest Highway before it ends.

This section of 3N17 is paved, but narrow, with rock slides here and there. A mountain bike's fat tires are not required to make the trip, but you'll make use of your low gears, since the climb is pretty constant. Follow 3N17 until you reach a gated road that branches off towards the actual summit of Magic Mountain. A Civil Air Defense station in Cold War times, the mountain now sports a crop of micro-wave dishes. Quite a view, here, isn't there? If the air is clear, you can see straight to the ocean over the San Gabriels, Santa Susannas, and Santa Monica Mountains. Turning north, you can look over the Saugus backcountry to the Tehachapi Mountains.

Road 3N17 continues east off the shoulder of Magic Mountain and drops down toward North Fork Ranger Station and Mt. Gleason. I have ridden from here to Mt. Gleason and back, and I can't say that I particularly enjoyed the 30-mile round trip. There were too many long pavement climbs that gave little reward for all the effort. There are better ways to get to Mt. Gleason, which are explored in other ride descriptions (see Chapter 6).

To return, retrace your route on 3N17 back to your vehicle, keeping an eyeball peeled for motor traffic.

Mendenhall Ridge to Iron Mountain

Trip Length: 22.6 miles
Time: 3+ hours
Difficulty: Moderately strenuous
Elevation Gain: 2,600'
Ride Type: Fire road out-and-back
Road Number: 3N32
Topo Map: Sunland, Condor Peak
Comments: This is a great one for riders seeking to get to the backcountry without working too hard. The grade is consistent and reasonable with some rocky sections to deal with. Nicely scenic.

Follow driving directions for the ride to Camp Nine. This ride starts where 3N32 meets Little Tujunga Canyon Road at Dillon Divide, a few miles southeast from the Bear Divide Rest Area. Road 3N32 is gated to vehicle traffic, so there is little chance of running into someone's 4X4. The road also goes west toward Kagel Mountain. It is not gated in that direction and is heavily used by hang gliders to access the top of Kagel Mountain. You want the east part of 3N32.

The grade you begin pedaling up is typical of the entire ride and, if anything, eases from here. At 0.3 mile, stay right. At 2.7 miles, you reach the intersection of 3N32 and 3N37. Stay left and continue on 3N32. At 2.8 miles, you reach the intersection of 3N32 and 4N35. This lower road on the left drops into Pacoima Canyon. Stay right and continue on 3N32. The ride is still nice and mellow and gets prettier as you go. At 4.7 miles, you cross from the northern side of Mendenhall

Ridge to the south side. Looking south, Little Tujunga Canyon snakes toward the city limits. Gold Creek Canyon is directly below, Yerba Buena Ridge across from you.

A road branches off to your right and climbs up to Mendenhall Peak, the name commemorating William Mendenhall, a National Forest supervisor. You may explore a deteriorating road that leads up to the top if you wish, but any mileage incurred is not included here.

Keeping left on 3N32, travelling gets more difficult. The road is covered with broken rocks the size of a hen's eggs, but you should be warmed up by now, and the scenery improves by the mile. You cruise along a ridge with alternating views north to south, and at 6.3 miles, you descend a little. At 6.9 miles, 13W02 comes in on the left. The trail is overgrown with poison oak and the entrance is difficult to find. At 8.9 miles, you reach the Yerba Buena Trail. The trail sign is largely illegible due to shotgun blasts. Note: The Yerba Buena Trail is not recommended. It is rough, rampant with ticks, and overgrown with brush and cactus. In addition, you would end up on Yerba Buena Ridge far below with no easy return.

Back on 3N32, the ride gets nicer and nicer, and by now you are quite far from the noise and rush of civilization. The temperature here should be noticeably cooler as you near the 5,000-foot level. Large conifers are scattered among the oaks, and in April you may still see large patches of snow in shaded areas. Grasses surround pale yellow blooms of sticky monkeyflower, and everything seems right with the world. Rolling around the north side of Iron Mountain at 11.3 miles or so, you can see down to Indian Ben Saddle and the confluence of roads from Pacoima Canyon and Mt. Gleason. This brings you to a decision point. If you turn around before you descend from Iron Mountain, it is a 12-mile descent, broken only by a few short climbs, back to your starting point.

If you want to continue farther on this route, see the Pacoima Canyon Loop ride below. It is also possible to continue to Mt. Gleason by way of 3N32 to Lightning Point Campground. This would add some climbing to the trip but would be quite a ride. Directions would be as follows: Descend on 3N32 to Indian Ben Saddle, which is easily distinguishable by the water tank at the crossroads. Keep straight ahead and to the right on 3N32 and climb towards Lightning Point Campground. About 3.5 miles up 3N32 you come to the campground, and 1.4 miles beyond it you reach 3N17. A right turn onto the pavement takes you up to Mt. Gleason. A left turn onto the dirt on 3N17 will take you to Messenger Flats Campground.

Mendenhall Ridge/Pacoima Canyon Loop

Trip Length: 27 miles
Time Allowed: 5+ hours
Difficulty: Very strenuous, very technical
Elevation Gain: 3,000'
Ride Type: Fire road, trail
Topo Map: Sunland, Condor Peak
Comments: Pacoima Canyon, once a shooting range and four-wheel-drive area, is now gated to motor vehicles and is technically closed to target shooters. Quite a few people with guns still go back here, however. This lovely canyon, shaded by sycamore and oak trees, shows a few scars of its past use, notably the rusting remains of an old Cadillac. There is an old roadbed that makes its way up the canyon and little by little becomes a trail. You can drop into Pacoima Canyon 0.3 mile north of Dillon Divide on 3N32 and explore up-canyon as far as you like. My favorite route through Pacoima Canyon is from the upper end with gravity as my friend. This makes the technically challenging, wet and rocky ride much more fun. There are lots and lots of water crossings—plan on getting your feet wet. Pacoima Canyon sees little use, so be careful.

Before attempting this ride, please check with the Forest Service on the condition of the trails. Pacoima Canyon sees little use, so it may not be in as good of shape as other routes in the area.

For this loop, follow the driving and riding instructions for the Mendenhall Ridge to Iron Mountain ride to mile 11.3, where you are looking east and down to Indian Ben Saddle. Take 3N32 down to the saddle and a junction at 12.5 miles, where 3N32, 3N31, Lightning Point

Trail, and the road to Trail Canyon and Condor Peak trails all come together.

Road 3N31 into Pacoima Canyon descends off to your left and behind you. Wide and easy to spot, it is still a road at this point. There will be no uphill for quite a while as you rush down into the canyon on an old path that is sometimes doubletrack, sometimes singletrack, and sometimes wide enough for vehicle travel. Whatever the case, it is always fun and I think you will enjoy it as much as I do. For miles you splash, bash, and bounce along through numerous rocks, fallen logs, and water crossings too numerous to count. At times the trail may seem to disappear, but keep heading downstream and it will always pick up again. Look for bits of trail flagging (red ribbon) tied to trees along the trail.

At 17.7 miles, the trail turns into a wide, graded road and continues down canyon. At 18.6 miles, bear left at the Y and climb above the creek for a little while only to return for more water crossings. At 21.3 miles, your road, now 4N35, climbs steeply out of the canyon and heads up to 3N32. It is a real grind, and reaches 3N32 after 2.8 hard miles. It is then a cruise back to the start for a total of 27 miles.

At one time 3N31 continued down canyon. To the right at the 4N35 junction leads, it dives over a small embankment and runs on. However, it soon degenerates into a bushwhacking portage. If the trail is ever restored, it would make a great finish for the loop, since this section of Pacoima Canyon is beautiful, full of oaks and sycamores. For now—believe it or not—it's easier to make the tough climb back up 4N35 to 3N32.

Trail Canyon Trail

Trip Length: 6.5 miles (trail only)
Time Allowed: 2 hours+
Difficulty: Strenuous, technical
Elevation Gain: 3,000', trail only
Ride Type: Out-and-back on trail
Road Number: 13W03
Topo Map: Sunland, Condor
Comments: Trail Canyon Trail underwent reconstruction by the U.S. Forest Service several years ago and is now clean and improved all the way on its climb from Big Tujunga Canyon Road through Tom Lucas Camp to Iron Mountain. The climb up is a workout and pushing is necessary. At the top, you could continue past Indian Ben Saddle to Lightning Point or Mt. Gleason, although this would be a tough 15 miles or so one way with over 4,000 feet of elevation gain.

To drive to the trailhead from Sunland, take the Sunland Avenue offramp from the 210. Make a left on Foothill Boulevard and a right on Big Tujunga Canyon Road.

0.0 mile. Beginning as a fire road on the north side of Big Tujunga Canyon Road about a half mile northwest of Vogel Flats Picnic Area and Big Tujunga Station, 13W03 at first is part of 3W29. Road 3W29 continues to the left and climbs a ridiculously steep grade up toward Yerba Buena Ridge, while 13W03 continues to the right and soon becomes a trail. After 4.8 miles, including more stairstep water bars than you'll care to remember, you come to Tom Lucas Camp.

The trail tops out where Condor Peak Trail heads east. Note: At this time Condor Peak Trail is not recommended for bicycle travel due to its high level of exposure and generally poor trail conditions. The fire road straight ahead climbs up to Indian Ben Saddle 1.1 mile away. To continue, keep right through the gate 0.7 mile from the trailhead at the road to Iron Mountain. After 0.4 mile you reach Indian Ben Saddle. Road 3N32, the one farthest right, climbs 3.5 miles up toward Lightning Point Campground.

Part II

The Saugus District
(Angeles National Forest)

and Mt. Pinos

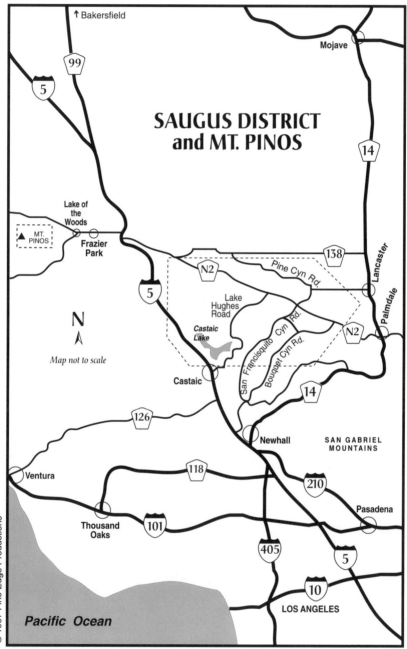

↑ Bakersfield

Mojave

99

5

SAUGUS DISTRICT and MT. PINOS

14

Lake of the Woods

MT. PINOS

Frazier Park

138

Lancaster

Pine Cyn Rd.

Palmdale

N2

5

Lake Hughes Road

N

Map not to scale

Castaic Lake

San Francisquito Cyn Rd.

Bouquet Cyn Rd.

N2

Castaic

14

126

Newhall

SAN GABRIEL MOUNTAINS

Ventura

118

210

Pasadena

Thousand Oaks

101

405

5

10

Pacific Ocean

LOS ANGELES

© 1997 Fine Edge Productions

Introduction

The northernmost section of Angeles National Forest, the Saugus District, has a different character than the rest of the Angeles—rounder and not so rocky and rugged, and lacking the elevation of the San Gabriels to the southeast. Still, the Saugus District has much to offer the mountain cyclist. The topography generally make for easier climbs, and the area is far less travelled than the heavily used San Gabriels.

The Liebre and Sawmill Mountains section of the Saugus District contain the best scenery and the highest elevations (5,000 feet plus), along with fine mountain biking possibilities. On an especially clear day, the top of 5,700-foot Burnt Peak can show you a glimmer of the distant Pacific Ocean. Sawmill and Upper Shake Campgrounds are two of the most beautiful campgrounds in the district, and the higher elevations of Sawmill Mountain bring with them large pine trees that whisper in the cooling breezes.

This area provided lumber for the construction of nearby Ft. Tejon, an early army establishment and key outpost along the trading route to the San Joaquin Valley to the east. Today, the Pacific Crest National Scenic Trail (closed to bikes) crosses much of the area.

At the northern tip of this range, Liebre Mountain (the name comes from the Spanish word for cottontail) shoulders fine stands of black oak woodland and is especially rewarding to ride in the fall when the leaves are turning color and carpeting the forest floor.

Summer temperatures are milder here than in the lower areas of the National Forest, but still expect highs into the upper nineties. There is no water available on the rides, so bring plenty with you. Winter can bring snow to Liebre and Sawmill, although this usually isn't heavy or long-lasting. The Saugus District lends itself to year-round exploration if you avoid the hottest days of summer and the coldest days of winter; spring and fall are particularly fine times to ride.

History of the Saugus District

In 1772, Pedro Fages, second in command to Gaspar de Portolá at the Presidio of San Diego, went looking for six of his men who had run off with some Indian women. He followed them up Castaic Canyon and past Quail Lake. He is credited with naming the Grapevine area "Cañada de Las Uvas" (canyon of the grapes). On this journey he found "high barren hills, difficult for beasts of burden." Could he have possibly envisioned mountain bikes?

The next person of any significance to travel the Fages route was a Franciscan friar, Padre Garces. Garces was quite the adventurer. He travelled on foot and hobnobbed with the Indians as he went. As you ride through these rugged canyons, think about Padre Garces passing through on foot, no fiberglass reinforced backpack, no compass, no map, and heaven forbid, not one piece of Goretex clothing!

In 1822, California passed into Mexican hands, and a good part of the Saugus District became Mexican land grants–Rancho Liebre, Rancho Tejon, and Rancho San Francisco. The drought of 1863-65 forced many landowners to move their herds to better grazing lands, and often they could not meet their mortgages.

Later, Edward F. Beale purchased the Liebre Grant for three cents an acre, and by 1868, he had amassed what is now the Tejon Ranch, a landholding of 265,000 acres.

In 1854, with the building of Ft. Tejon, traffic through the area increased. General Beale ran a supply train of camels to the fort. Along the same route, Phineas Banning brought passengers and freight to Fort Tejon by wagon. The route followed the old Indian and Spanish trade paths and wound its way up Elizabeth Lake Canyon, crossed Pine Canyon to the northeast, and passed through the Quail Lake area before turning toward Tejon. With the outbreak of the Civil War, the U.S. Army abandoned Fort Tejon. Today the fort is open to the public as a site of historical interest.

"Bad guys" found their reasons to come to the Saugus District, too. Tiburcio Vasquez, the famed Mexican bandit after whom Vasquez Rocks County Park is named, haunted the area of Elizabeth Lake and Pine Canyon and would stay at a relative's ranch located nearby. It was a wilder place at that time. There were grizzly bears in the mountains and antelope were plentiful on the plains.

In later decades, scattered mining interests popped up through the district. The washes of San Francisquito and other canyons provided some placering interests, and there is at least one working gold mine still in operation. The St. Francis Dam collapse of 1928 washed away enough streamed and topsoil to renew interest in prospecting the washes of San Francisquito Canyon, and during the Depression, the area was once again busy with gold pans and dry washers.

Antelope are no longer found in these parts and the grizzly bear is long gone. The footsteps of the Franciscan padres have faded into time, as have the creaking wagon wheels and the odd gruntings of camels ridden by weary cavalrymen. Ever encroaching civilization is changing the look of the boundaries of Angeles National Forest, but the forest itself is largely unchanged, waiting for modern-day Beales and Fages to explore its ranges.

Natural History of the Saugus District

From pine forests to oak woodlands and creekside glens, you'll find several different life zones within the Saugus District. The vast majority of the area is chaparral, however, the predominant vegetation found in the Southern California mountains up to elevations of 5,000 feet.

The chaparral includes a wide variety of plant life, and all species are well adapted to the semi-arid conditions found here (average annual rainfall is from 5 to 15 inches). Although rarely attaining more than 6 feet in height, the brush can be impenetrable at times—ask anyone who has tried to travel cross-country through these foothills. Most shrubs are evergreen with small, leathery leaves evolved to withstand drought and fire. The most common plants are chamise (greasewood) and whitethorn (buckbrush or deerbrush). Yucca, manzanita, scrub oak, and mountain mahogany are all common chaparral plants, with redberry, flannel bush, sugar bush, and buckwheat less common. And, let's not forget poison oak.

It is not all brush; many bright-colored flowers grow here. Tree tobacco is common, and you will find Indian paintbrush, prickly phlox, the less common wooly blue curls, and the brilliant California poppy.

A busy animal community thrives within the dense cover of chaparral. Mule deer are common, but they are shy and not easily seen. However, the relatively silent, swift approach of a mountain bike allows quite a few encounters with them, particularly early and late in the day. Coyote, bobcat, and raccoons are here, as well as California quail, red-tailed hawks, and scrub jays. Hugging the ground are plenty of lizards, an occasional tarantula, and enough rattlesnakes to keep you on guard. Bees are a crucial part of the chaparral habitat, and in spring and summer you find them in countless numbers. On a trip through the San Gabriel Mountains, naturalist John Muir commented that "... from the highest summit, far as the eye could reach, the landscape was one vast bee-pasture, a rolling wilderness of honey-bloom."

Another primary habitat is the riparian or stream-side zone, areas of year-round or seasonal water flow. The presence of water, a rare commodity in the Saugus District, makes this a key habitat for flora and fauna. Willows and cottonwoods are the dominant trees, and you will also see live oaks, big leaf maple, sycamore, white alder, and mulefat. Cattails, bullrushes, sedges, and watercress can be found in and along streams, ponds, and springs. The varied animal life includes deer, raccoons, skunks, woodrats, opossum, kingfishers, rufous-sided towhees, yellow warblers, western flycatchers, house wrens, garter snakes, pond turtles, toads, rainbow trout, and mosquito fish. Bouquet Creek, Piru Creek, and the Cienaga Camp areas are good examples of the riparian zone. This type of habitat is the most visited and, unfortunately, the most easily affected.

Heading up out of the southern drainages above the chaparral, you come to the oak woodland zone. Found at elevations between 5,000 and 7,500 feet, the oak woodland is noticeably distinct from the lower chaparral. The increase in elevation brings with it cooler temperatures and a moister climate with yearly snowfall. Liebre Mountain (5,760') has a fine example of oak woodland, but since the Saugus Range is mostly below 5,000 feet, this is not a common habitat in this section of Angeles National Forest.

At the higher elevations, such as on Sawmill Mountain, grand ponderosa and digger pines take their stand. Big cone Douglas fir can be found scattered among the pines in the draws and canyons, particularly the north-facing drainages on upper Liebre Mountain. Incense cedars also add their fragrance to the mix. Although coastal and interior live oaks grow here, the black oak is dominant. A deciduous tree, its leaves and bark are quite different from the other oaks. Look for grasses beneath them and mistletoe in the trees. Bushy-tailed tree squirrels mix with the more common ground squirrel, and you'll also see chipmunks, chickadees, acorn woodpeckers, kingsnakes, and the ever-present mule deer. Don't be surprised to see the tracks of mountain lion or bear, but it's not likely you will spy the animals that left them. Look up in the sky, too. Golden eagles pass through the Liebre Mountain area, and with the 1988 release of Andean condors to the Piru and Pyramid areas, spotting a condor is not out of the question.

Keep in mind that these different zones mix together, and their boundaries are not as cut and dried as they are on paper. Also, with the experimental planting that the Forest Service has done through the years, you can never be quite sure what you will find in the planted groves. If you see a pine tree surrounded by whitethorn, don't blame us, we just ride here!

CHAPTER 9

Bouquet Canyon

The Bouquet Canyon area offers a variety of recreational opportunities. Bouquet Creek, which flows out of Bouquet Reservoir, is one of only two creeks of any size in the Saugus District that flow year-round, and it is regularly stocked with rainbow trout. (Bouquet Reservoir, however, is closed to public use.) The Big Oaks Lodge in Bouquet Canyon dates back to the 1920s as a popular party spot and was built by the man who also built the first commercial building in the canyon in the area now called "The Falls." The lodge is now a restaurant and bar.

In the early days, people would come into the canyon by wagon or on foot and meet for community dances and other get-togethers. The houses that line the creek in some areas were built primarily as vacation cabins back in the '20s and '30s. The Falls campground is a popular spot to visit. A short hike upstream from the campground brings you to a lovely waterfall with some wading pools underneath. Sadly, trash and graffiti have spoiled this experience.

It is not uncommon for snow to fall in the canyon, and past the reservoir snowfall can be quite heavy. Be cautious of heavy traffic on weekend days when waders, fishermen, and others all compete for space.

There is no water provided at campgrounds. Creek water is unsuitable for drinking, so be sure to carry an adequate supply.

Sierra Pelona Ridge

Trip Length: 7.6 miles
Time Allowed: 90 minutes
Difficulty: Strenuous; nontechnical
Elevation Gain: 1,400'
Ride Type: Fire road in and out with loop options
Road Number: 6N08 to the top
Topo Map: Sleepy Valley
Comments: This road accesses a fine riding area. The Sierra Pelona is a pretty, windswept landscape dotted with oaks. Road 6N08 takes you to the beginning of the ride, and the end of the ride is the starting point for many other routes in this chapter. Watch out for OHV traffic. Plan on wind and cooler temperatures on the ridge than at your starting point.

From Highway 14 take Palmdale Boulevard west (N2), which becomes Elizabeth Lake Road. Continue to Bouquet Canyon Road, turn left, and follow over the hill to 6N08 on the left. If you are coming from Los Angeles heading north on I-5, take the Valencia Boulevard exit and drive east. At Bouquet Canyon Road turn left (north). Drive up Bouquet Canyon Road past the reservoir's dam site and find road 6N08 on the right.

Road 6N08 takes off from Bouquet Canyon Road just a little to the east of the dam overlook at Bouquet Canyon Reservoir. It is not marked but is easily found. A good parking spot is located 100 yards up 6N08, at a wide area where 6N06 comes in.

Start along 6N08 on a nice downhill grade that ends all too soon. At a sharp right turn, you begin climbing toward the backbone of the Sierra Pelona. This is a hot ride in summer, and the only shade you can find is at 2.0 miles when you roll past Artesian Springs. Not marked by any sign, Artesian Springs is located to the right of the road and is liberally sprinkled with oaks and crisscrossed with motorcycle paths. This spot is used as a base camp by many motorcyclists, and you can do the same if you wish.

Continuing up 6N08, the route steepens somewhat. At 3.8 miles, bear left. At 4.4 miles, you pop over onto a saddle on Sierra Pelona Ridge. This junction with 6N07 is the turning point of the ride, but by referring to other rides in this chapter, you can ride all day here. Enjoy the view. You worked for it.

To return to your vehicle, simply retrace your route down an enjoyable 4-mile descent. Again, look out for OHV traffic.

Sierra Pelona Loop

Trip Length: 23.5 miles
Time Allowed: 2 to 3 hours, plus time for options
Elevation Gain: 2,600'
Difficulty: Strenuous and nontechnical, but options are technical
Ride Type: Fire road and pavement, with trail option
Road Numbers: 6N07, 6N08, Bouquet Canyon Road
Topo Maps: Sleepy Valley, Green Valley

Compared to riding up 6N08 to 6N07, as described in the previous ride, this is by far the more challenging way to access the Sierra Pelona, due to the long and sustained climb. It is a great loop, though, and a real workout. The downhill on the flip side of the ridge is great, and the pavement return is easy and scenic. If Five Deer Trail is added to the fun, this ride sparkles for the fit rider.

Road 6N07 meets Bouquet Canyon Road 1.8 miles north of the Texas Canyon Forest Service station. There is a parking area on the west side of the paved road. The ride starts by heading east on 6N07, which immediately begins the long ascent toward Sierra Pelona Ridge. Sit in and pedal as the road switchbacks up to the first summit at 2.0 miles. Here, at a water tank, 6N07 turns left and you get your first view of the San Gabriels—a panorama from Bear Divide at Sand Canyon to Mt. Pacifico in the east.

At 4.5 miles, another summit grants you a short descent. At 5.8 miles, road 5N18, originating from Rowher Flat OHV area, comes in from the right. Keep riding straight ahead on 6N07 and continue to climb. A few ups-and-downs bring you to a wooded area (oaks) at 9.4 miles, which signals the beginning of the end of the long ascent. The main road is intersected in several areas by 4WD roads, which are easily discerned.

At 10.9 miles, after a welcome downhill, you reach 6N08. Here you have a choice of several paths. For the simplest return, go left on 6N08 for an immediate downhill charge to Bouquet Canyon Road at 16.25 miles. Then turn left and enjoy a pleasant pedal on pavement, following the winding stream. The parking area is reached at 23.5 miles.

You can add to the ride in several ways:

1) Follow 6N07 east along Sierra Pelona Ridge beyond the 6N08 junction toward Mt. McDill. It is rough and hilly, but a good ride.

From the trail's end near Mt. McDill, retrace your route to return.

2) Return down 6N07 the way you came up. Remember all the up you just did? Flip it over and whaddya get? A long, fast, yahoooo descent. Watch for oncoming motorcycles and other trail users!

3) Add Five Deer Trail to the loop. This is highly recommended if you are not too tired. It adds a little technical work and a whole lot of fun. See the Five Deer Loop ride below for directions from the 6N07/6N08 intersection.

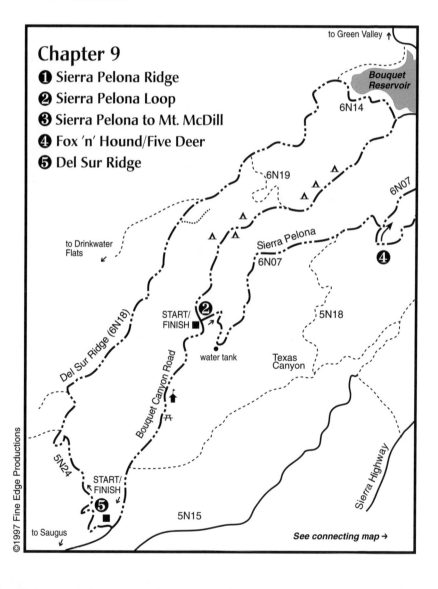

Sierra Pelona to Mt. McDill

Trip Length: 16.8 miles, or 17.6 miles with trail option
Time Allowed: 3.5 hours, or 4 hours with trail option
Difficulty: Strenuous; rough road adds some technical areas. Trail option includes technical singletrack.
Elevation Gain: 1,700'
Ride Type: Fire road out-and-back with trail option
Road Number: 6N08
Topo Map: Sleepy Valley

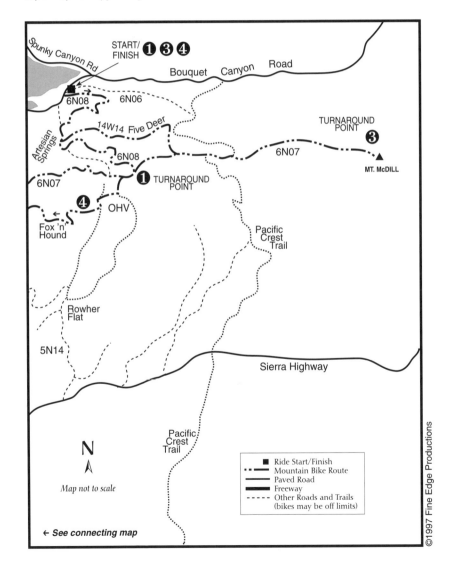

© 1997 Fine Edge Productions

Comments: This is a very good climb with great views of the high desert area to the north and the San Gabriel Mountains to the south. The rough character of the fire road makes this a challenging descent. Beware of OHV users. You can use Five Deer Trail as an alternate return.

From Highway 14 take Palmdale Boulevard west (N2), which becomes Elizabeth Lake Road. Continue to Bouquet Canyon Road, turn left, and follow over the hill to 6N08 on the left. If you are coming from Los Angeles heading north on I-5, take the Valencia Boulevard exit and drive east. At Bouquet Canyon Road turn left (north). Drive up Bouquet Canyon Road past the reservoir's dam site and find road 6N08 on the right, just a little to the east of the dam overlook at Bouquet Canyon Reservoir. It is not marked but is easily found. A good parking spot is found 100 yards up 6N08, at a wide area where 6N06 comes in.

From here, begin riding by heading to the right on ungated 6N08. Descend a short distance before making a hard right. Then start climb-ing. Road 6N08 is rough and rocky as it climbs toward the top. As you ascend, you roll through some small oak groves; the blue waters of Bouquet Reservoir stretch below you to the west.

At 2.0 miles you pass Artesian Springs Camp. From here the road leaves the lower oak groves and continues to climb in long stages to the junction with 6N07 at 4.4 miles. Looking south, you can see the northern slopes of the San Gabriel Mountains.

To the east is tower-crowned Mt. McDill. Ride east on 6N07, which is crisscrossed several times by motorcycle paths, and just keep to the main route. Road 6N07 rollercoasters with fast descents followed by short, steep climbs. At 8.4 miles you come to a locked gate (private property), and your turnaround point.

There are two options for the return. You can retrace your route back to the junction with 6N08 for a long, fast descent to the base of Sierra Pelona. For a fun and challenging singletrack, turn right at 11.6 miles onto unmarked Five Deer Trail. This singletrack runs across Sierra Pelona to rejoin Road 6N08 at Artesian Springs Campground. Then turn right and descend on 6N08 to return to your vehicle.

Fox 'n' Hound–Five Deer Trail

Trip Length: 19.6 miles
Time Allowed: 5 hours
Difficulty: Strenuous, with technical singletrack sections
Elevation Gain: 1,600'
Ride Type: Fire road and singletrack figure eight
Topo Map: Sleep Valley and Green Valley
Comments: The ride combining Five Deer Trail (14W14) with Fox 'n' Hound reflects the personal preference of coauthor Kevin Woten and is a very challenging and enjoyable hammerfest as such. Five Deer Trail has been a favorite of his since 1985, and several years ago he expanded his ride to include the fire road up Sierra Pelona Mountain and an unnamed motorcycle trail on the south side of Sierra Pelona. This resulted in the figure-eight loop described here. The good fire road climb, two different but challenging trails, and the fire road descent test your all-around cross-country skills. At a slower pace, this makes a good training ride or day excursion.

Most folks, however, find Five Deer Trail challenging enough without the additional loop. To do this simpler ride, turn left at the junction with 6N07 (at 4.4 miles) and pick up the ride text three paragraphs from the end of this description at "Ahead waits more singletrack."

Drive and park as described in the Sierra Pelona to Mt. McDill ride above. This route follows that ride up 6N08 to the 4.4-mile point, at the junction with 6N07.

The 6N08/6N07 junction is a good spot to catch your breath. Looking to the south, you can see Vasquez Rocks and the small town of Aqua Dulce below. Farther south stand the northern ramparts of the San Gabriel Mountains. If you decide just to do Five Deer Trail, you turn left here. To do Fox 'n' Hound, however, you turn right (west) on 6N07.

Climb 0.1 mile on 6N07 and turn left (south) onto the OHV road that heads toward Rowher Flats. This is the beginning of Fox 'n' Hound. The trail is signed "Most Difficult." Ride 200 feet down the rocky, rutted OHV road, then turn right onto the signed OHV trail. Roll along the slope to reach another OHV trail at 5.4 miles. Go left and descend steeply to pick up the trail again at 5.6 miles. Go right on the well-ridden trail, which winds across the side of Sierra Pelona Mountain. There is plenty of rock here and full concentration is needed to pick lines through short, steep climbs and long, rutted drops. (This is a great technical trail and is a good warmup for Moab.)

At 8.1 miles, you reach unsigned 5N18 and the end of Fox 'n' Hound Trail. Turn right and climb to 6N07 directly above you. Go right again and grind up toward Sierra Pelona Summit. Soon you top out and reach the site of an old Forest Service tower, of which only a few blocks of the foundation remain. Go east again on 6N07, rolling a bit and then descending to the junction with 6N08.

Ahead awaits more singletrack! Roll easily east along Sierra Pelona Ridge, staying on 6N07. At 13.2 miles, go left onto Five Deer Trail (14W14). The trail drops down the slope onto an old motorcycle track. Ride down the rutted, rocky trail past grass-covered knolls on the mountain's north side. Many motorcycle trails crisscross your route, but stay on the main trail and descend rapidly. At 13.7 miles, take the second left (west). The trail has a series of motorcycle jumps and whoops before it drops steeply to the north. At the bottom of the drop, go hard left and ride down to the edge of the chaparral. From this point you head west. First, though, you can take the trail to the right for 0.3 mile to view the remains of the Big Oak—the world's largest recorded canyon live oak before fire destroyed it years ago. The tree's remains are still quite impressive—nearly as thick as a mature redwood in girth. A small spring bubbles from the foot of the tree, almost as though life still flows from it. Return the 0.3 mile up the trail to the Five Deer junction.

Go right (west) at the junction and climb a bit before rolling across the mountainside. Five Deer is a sharp contrast to the previous trail: brushy, shaded, and downhill for the most part. This is a very popular route, with tight chutes, turns, and rutted descents. Watch for poison oak, which is abundant here. At 17.6 miles you cross an OHV trail that climbs the mountain. Continue 0.2 mile to rejoin 6N08 at Artesian Springs Camp. Then turn right on 6N08 and head down the mountain to your vehicle.

Del Sur Ridge

Trip Length: 17.8 miles
Time Allowed: 3 hours
Difficulty: Moderately strenuous due to one steep climb; nontechnical
Elevation Gain: 1,800'
Ride Type: Loop, fire road and pavement mix
Road Number: 5N24, 6N18, 6N19
Topo Maps: Green Valley, Mint Canyon
Comments: This is an enjoyable loop, and with the exception of some steep climbing, is not too difficult. A hot ride in the summer, it's best to start early in the day.

Coming north on I-5 from Los Angeles, take Valencia Boulevard east to Bouquet Canyon Road in Saugus. Turn left and drive up Bouquet Canyon Road past Vasquez Canyon Road to the intersection with Road 5N24. Coming from Highway 14, take Sand Canyon exit north. Turn right on Sierra Highway and continue about a half-mile to Vasquez Canyon Road. Turn left and continue to Bouquet Canyon Road. It is about three-quarters of a mile to 5N24 on the left.

At the 5N24 junction, a sign under some pepper trees reads *Coarse Gold Rd/Del Sur Rd 3 Miles*. Park here and start riding up 5N24, which begins by heading southwest. This first section is on private property, so stay on the road. Before long, you pass a dog kennel. The sound of barking, teeth-baring animals made our calves cringe, but don't worry. A tall chain link fence separates them from thee. Continue on your way as the road climbs and drops until, at 2.1 miles, you reach a gated road on the left. This leads to Haskell Canyon, which is private property. Your route continues to the right (northeast) past the sign for Del Sur Quarry Road.

Now you have to work for a while to gain any ground. The grade increases as you ride toward the summit of the trip, about 3,500 feet, which is reached at about 4 miles. The view from here on a clear day toward the south (looking toward the Santa Clarita Valley) is very nice and is some comfort to your tired legs. All the hard work is over at this point. The road follows the ridge and rolls along with no significant elevation change and only some small hills to conquer. *Caution:* At 6.9 miles you pass a mining operation (stone quarry), and from this point on you will have to be on the lookout for large, noisy trucks. You reach another spur road at 7.3 miles that takes off to the left and drops into Drinkwater Flat from the top. This is a designated OHV trail and is easily distinguished from the main road. At 8.7 miles you take the right road (east) past a cistern and start the downhill section of the fire road. You drop fast and reach Bouquet Canyon Road in no time. With 11.2 miles showing on the computer and some warm brake pads, you find yourself back at the paved road. Turn right.

The return leg of the trip on Bouquet Canyon Road is an easy all-downhill cruise. Bouquet Canyon Road is popular with road riders, and the time you spend on it will show you why. A stream and large sycamore and oak trees make for a pleasant passage. Campground areas beckon tired feet and dusty faces with a chance to play in the cool stream water. On weekend days, Bouquet Canyon Road sees heavy traffic and can be surprisingly busy with fishermen and others enjoying the creek. At 17.8 miles you are back at your vehicle.

CHAPTER 10

San Francisquito Canyon and Green Valley

St. Francis Loop

Trip Length: 8.1 miles
Time Allowed: 60 to 90 minutes
Difficulty: Moderate
Elevation Gain: 600'
Ride Type: Loop; fire road and pavement mix
Road Numbers: 5N16, 5N17, 5N30
Topo Map: Warm Springs Mountain
Comments: On this reasonable beginner ride—not too long or too difficult—you pass the site of collapsed St. Francis Dam. San Francisquito Canyon has the unfortunate distinction of being the site of one of the worst disasters in California history. On March 12, 1928, at 11:57 p.m., a newly constructed dam holding 12 billion gallons of water gave way, unleashing a torrent of death and destruction that ran all the way to the Pacific Ocean, over 60 miles away. In the process, 450 people were killed by a wall of water that was estimated to be 140 feet high for the first few miles down the canyon.

The dam was engineered by William Mulholland, the man who brought Owens Valley water to the city of Los Angeles with his aqueduct system. All that remains of the dam now are large chunks of dun-colored material that were carried down the canyon and some rubble at the dam site itself.

Despite the fact that the canyon's history is accented by a flood disaster, there is no water available along the rides. So plan ahead and bring all you will need for the day.

Take I-5 to Valencia Boulevard, go east to Bouquet Canyon Road, and turn left. Take Bouquet Canyon Road about a mile to a signal at Seco Canyon Road. Turn left and follow this road to a stop sign at San Francisquito Canyon Road/Copperhill Drive. Turn left. It is about 6 miles along San Francisquito Canyon Road to 5N30, where this ride begins. If you are starting from Highway 14, take San Fernando Road north through old Newhall to where it becomes Bouquet Canyon Road (at the junction with Valencia Boulevard). Continue to the ride start by following the driving instructions above from Bouquet Canyon Road.

This route can be ridden in either direction, but this is the more popular way.

Where 5N30 (the road through Dry Gulch) intersects San Francisquito Canyon Road, park in the large dirt area. Ride northwest on 5N30 into Dry Gulch Canyon. (There is a gated dirt road that parallels San Francisquito Canyon Road and returns down canyon. Avoid this and follow 5N30 to the right.) Now a pleasant little section to ride, the road through Dry Gulch crosses a small creek and follows a steadily climbing course toward Lake Hughes Road. A few years ago this was a designated shooting area littered with bullet-riddled cans, refrigerators, and whatever else people hauled in to shoot, and the incessant sound of gunfire would have accompanied you on your ride. Cleaned up and closed to shooting, this little arroyo has returned to a peaceful state.

At 1.4 miles, after a steep, short climb, you reach an intersection where you take 5N17 to the left and begin climbing in earnest. The road is a granny ring to all but the most fit. It's the hardest part of the ride, and if you survive, you're good to 60!

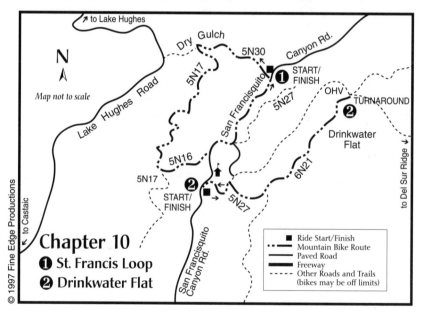

Chapter 10

❶ St. Francis Loop
❷ Drinkwater Flat

When you top out, swing to the right and follow the fire road as it rollercoasters its way down the ridge line. At 3.6 miles, turn left onto 5N16, a fire road that plummets down to San Francisquito Canyon. (Road 5N17 continues south, but it leads to private property at a county jail facility.)

After a creek crossing, you meet San Francisquito Canyon Road. Turn left on the pavement and head up canyon, watching out for cars. Almost immediately you pass San Francisquito Ranger Station, then a power station. Soon you can see large chunks of dam rubble lying in the creek bed. Then as you climb over a steep rise in the pavement, look to the right at the remains of St. Francis Dam. At 8.1 miles you arrive back at your parked vehicle.

Drinkwater Flat

Trip Length: Varies, 8+ miles
Time Allowed: Varies
Difficulty: Moderate
Elevation Gain: 500'
Ride Type: Fire road with trail and exploration options
Road Numbers: 5N27, 6N21
Topo Maps: Warm Springs Mountain, Green Valley
Comments: This is a popular area for four-wheelers, motorcyclists, and mountain bicyclists. The flat is a grassy meadow tucked between Del Sur Ridge and San Francisquito Canyon Road. In earlier times, Indians came here to hunt, gather acorns, and trade with other villages and tribes. In more recent times, prospectors and miners dug the surrounding hills in search of gold. Today Drinkwater Flat is crisscrossed with numerous motorcycle and off-highway vehicle trails. The Forest Service requests that cyclists check in with them before entering this area.

Follow the driving directions in the St. Francis Loop ride above to San Francisquito Canyon Road. It is about 5 miles along San Francisquito Canyon Road to the junction with 5N27, the start of this ride. Park at the gated roadhead.

Ride past the gate 0.3 mile to a junction. Keep right and climb the old paved road. For about the first quarter mile the road climbs, but then it levels out and is nearly flat for the next 3 miles. Below and on your right, you can see San Francisquito Canyon Road and the gullied hillsides of Red Mountain.

It is hard to imagine that all this was under water, but this was the lake bed of the St. Francis Reservoir. In fact, as you ride along the road you can see the old foundations of the dam just south of Dry

Gulch Canyon. The foundations of several old houses come into view at 3.4 miles. Just beyond, the huge pipes of the Los Angeles Aqueduct emerge from the ground for a hundred feet and then tunnel back into the hillside like giant earthworms.

A small dam lies on your left at 3.5 miles. You descend past the dam and roll gradually up to Drinkwater Flat. At 4.0 miles you reach an OHV road. Pass the road and keep left at the next intersection. At 4.1 miles, you reach the junction with 6N21.

You are now in the center of Drinkwater Flat. Crisscrossing the road north and south are numerous singletracks. Riding the many jumps, gully crossings, and small knolls is like being on a rollercoaster. The meadow is small enough to be explored in several hours and large enough that you don't feel crowded, even with the motorcycles and four-wheelers. It's a good idea to bring extra water and food so you won't be limited in your explorations. Please stay on the trails and fire roads; do not travel crosscountry. When you have finished, return to your vehicle the way you came.

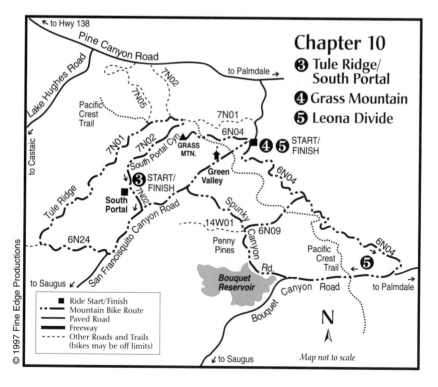

Tule Ridge/South Portal Loop

Trip Length: 20 miles
Time Allowed: 2+ hours
Difficulty: Strenuous with fast fire road sections
Elevation Gain: 1,800'
Ride Type: Loop on fire road and pavement
Road Number: 7N02, 6N24, 7N01
Topo Map: Lake Hughes
Comments: A fine training ride, Tule Ridge offers good views of the Saugus backcountry. South Portal Canyon is one of the best downhills in the area.

Follow driving instructions for the St. Francis Loop, but continue northeast up San Francisquito Canyon Road about 5 miles past the junction with 5N30 to Road 7N02. Begin the ride at old South Portal Campground, located a mile up 7N02. The campground is gone, but the shade of any oak tree off the main road will do for parking. (If you begin to ascend sharply as you look for parking, you have gone too far.)

This ride can be done in either direction, but as described here, you finish with a marvelous downhill into South Portal.

From the campground, ride back 1 mile to San Francisquito Canyon Road and turn right on the pavement. A fast downhill past a section of aqueduct pipe brings you to mile 5.0 and the beginning of Road 6N24, where you turn right. Located at the base of the downhill past the water pipes, 6N24 drops away to the right and splashes through a creek before laboring uphill toward Tule Ridge. Prepare to work a while on the uphill! At mile 5.1 you reach a saddle at Ruby Canyon. Turn right onto 7N01 and continue climbing up Tule Ridge. (Road 6N24 continues over the hill straight ahead toward Lake Hughes Road.)

Although many OHV paths cut into the road, the main route is obvious. Enjoy the ride and persevere, keeping right as you pass 7N05 at 7.1 miles. Descend to a saddle above South Portal Canyon where 7N02, 7N01, and 6N04 intersect. Bear right and drop into South Portal Canyon on 7N02, a rollicking hoot of a ride. Use caution and be sure to watch the blind corners for vehicle traffic. These 3 miles of joy bring you back to South Portal and your vehicle.

Grass Mountain

Trip Length: 5.6 miles
Time Allowed: 90 minutes
Difficulty: Mildly strenuous; nontechnical
Elevation Gain: 880'
Ride Type: Out-and-back on fire road
Road Number: 6N04
Topo Map: Lake Hughes
Comments: A fine view from the top and an easy climb make this a good short ride with a few steep sections. This is a pleasant after-work ride and is good for beginners. It is usually breezy at the top, even when it isn't down below, so be sure to carry a light windbreaker.

This ride and the next two are located in Green Valley, an area full of quality rides. You can make many good loops from the valley's fire roads. Fire burned large parts of Green Valley in 1989, but the riding is still just as good, and time will cover the scars made by the fire. It may snow in this area in winter, although the snow never stays on the ground very long. Carry all the water you will need with you, since none is available while you ride.

Follow driving instructions for the St. Francis Loop, but continue northeast up San Francisquito Canyon Road about 8 miles beyond the junction with 5N30. The ride starts at the junction with 6N04, 0.8 mile beyond the Green Valley Ranger Station on San Francisquito Canyon Road. Park where the sign reads *Grass Mountain, South Portal, Tule Ridge.*

Ride 6N04 west and begin climbing. As you head toward the mountaintop, you enjoy some great views of San Francisquito Canyon to the south.

The grade changes from mild to medium, but the entire climb is quite manageable and enjoyable. As you continue to climb, you roll around to the north side where parts of Antelope Valley come into view. At 1.8 miles, you come to a split in the road. Take the left-most route and continue climbing. (The right path takes you to South Portal/Tule Ridge.) The road gets steeper as you continue to the top, and at 2.8 miles you are there! The top of Grass Mountain is a good place to sit and watch the day wind down, and yes, it is grassy on top. In the winter, there is occasional snow on the mountain, but the road is usually negotiable even then.

Sierra Pelona and Bouquet Canyon are visible in the east. Over the top of the Sierra Pelona you can plainly see Mt. Gleason along with many other mountains in that range. Explore the west end of the top of Grass Mountain to get a good view of the Tule Ridge area and the road that runs along it. (As with many of these rides, the Pacific Crest Trail crosses your path. This trail is off limits to mountain bikes in its entirety. Please do not ride it.)

To return, just retrace your route downhill. Use caution since this road sees motor vehicle use at times.

Leona Divide

Trip Length: 23.5 miles
Time Allowed: 2+ hours
Difficulty: Strenuous; nontechnical
Elevation Gain: 1,700'
Ride Type: Fire road and pavement loop
Road Number: 6N04
Topo Maps: Lake Hughes, Green Valley, Sleepy Valley
Comments: This long loop begins easily but requires some horsepower to complete.

This ride begins at the same location as the Grass Mountain route described above.

From the intersection of 6N04 and San Francisquito Canyon Road, ride east and pass the sign that reads *Leona Divide Rd., Spunky Cyn. Rd. 5 mi., Bouquet Cyn. Rd. 12 mi.* Begin climbing an easy grade that offers some fine views of the valley below. The road steepens for a while, but soon tops out. At 2.9 miles, bear left, avoiding the OHV road to the right. You descend now, until at 4.0 miles you reach the intersection of 6N09 and 6N04. Continue ahead on 6N04 and begin climbing once again.

For a few miles the road follows along the Leona Divide, rising and falling enough to keep you using your gears. Some of the climbs work you fairly hard until, at 6.7 miles, the route levels out and gives you a chance to roll along and appreciate the view you've been anticipating. At 8.2 miles, you start a nearly 3-mile descent that takes you to Bouquet Canyon Road at 11 miles.

Turn right on Bouquet Canyon Road (paved) and start the return leg. Pedaling is easy and the surroundings are pleasant as you make your way toward the intersection of Bouquet Canyon Road and Spunky Canyon Road (also paved). At 14.2 miles, turn right and proceed along Spunky Canyon Road, riding along the backside of Bouquet Reservoir. This small lake is used only for drinking water and is closed to recreation.

The road soon begins the steep, winding climb over Spunky

Saddle. Watch for traffic—the road is quite narrow. At 17 miles, you reach the top at the Penny Pines Plantation.

Here you have a choice on how to continue. For the dirt return from Spunky Saddle, turn right up 6N09, directly across the street from Penny Pines Plantation. Crawl up to 6N04 and the Leona Divide (19.5 miles). Then turn left on 6N04 and retrace your route back to your vehicle.

To take the easier pavement return, continue on Spunky Canyon Road through the town of Green Valley, where you can buy snacks at a small store. At 19.7 miles you reach San Francisquito Canyon Road. Turn right and ride the remaining 2.3 miles (with some steep but short hills) back to your vehicle at 22 miles.

CHAPTER 11

Warm Springs Mountain and Cienaga Camp

Warm Springs Mountain

Trip Length: 12.6 miles
Time Allowed: 3 hours
Difficulty: Very technical and exposed
Elevation Gain: 1,600'
Ride Type: Fire road out-and-back
Road Numbers: 6N32, 7N13
Topo Map: Warm Springs Mountain
Comments: This is a big climb for these parts of Angeles National Forest, and the close proximity to Castaic makes it popular as a workout ride. The climb offers little in the way of rest, so as you ride you know it guarantees a long downhill on the return trip. Gravity: what a concept.

From the town of Castaic, Lake Hughes Road winds its way uphill, passes Castaic Lake, and heads north toward the communities of Lake Hughes and Lake Elizabeth. Just past Castaic Lake, which is very busy on most weekends, stands Warm Springs Mountain. At 4,020 feet, it is the tallest mountain in this section, and the tough climb to the summit rewards you with great views of the Santa Clarita Valley and beyond. An abandoned lookout tower, destroyed in the Ruby Canyon fire of 1987, sits on top of Warm Springs Mountain. The block building that remains is used as a weather station. Although still shown on the Forest Service map, Warm Springs Campground no longer exists. Badly damaged in the Ruby Canyon fire, it was later razed by the Forest Service. Warm Springs Rehabilitation Center is owned and operated by the County of Los Angeles and is off-limits to visitors.

To reach the start of this ride from Castaic (on I-5), go north on Lake Hughes Road 11 miles to the Warm Springs Rehabilitation

Center. Park in the pullouts on the side of the road and ride west on road 6N32 through the oak-forested canyon bottom. At 0.9 mile you begin more serious climbing and can see the fire-scarred north side of Warm Springs Mountain and part of your ascent winding high above. At 2.7 miles you reach the three-way junction, where you take the left road (7N13) up Warm Springs Mountain. Although this is a longer climb than from Lake Hughes Road to the junction, the grade is not as steep. As you climb, you can see Bouquet Reservoir in the east, Cobblestone Mountain in the west, and Burnt Peak to the north.

At 6.0 miles you roll onto the northern shoulder of Warm Springs Mountain. Continue to a junction and a gate at 6.2 miles. Above you are the remains of Warm Springs Mountain Lookout, and below to the west is the grassy bowl of Necktie Basin. Continue left past a gate and up a very short distance to the top and the old lookout tower site. Please don't play on the structure. (Remember Humpty Dumpty?) This is a great spot to look over the Santa Clarita Valley to the west and

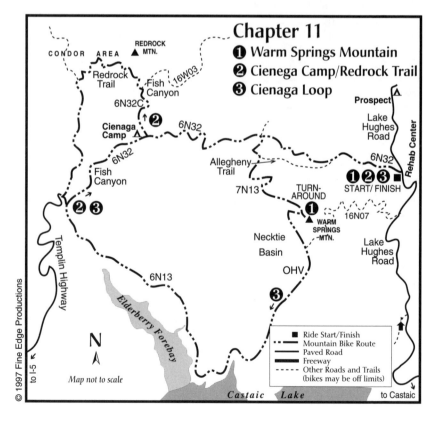

beyond; it rewards your hard efforts well.

Speaking of rewards, the return awaits with nearly 7 miles of constant down, down, down. As you noticed on the long climb, the first few miles off the top can be rocky, so have fun but ride smart. Retrace your steps down 7N13 to the three-way junction, where you bear right and continue on 6N32 back to your starting point.

Cienaga Camp/Redrock Trail

Trip Length: 14 miles round trip to Cienaga Camp and back; 9.5 miles for the Redrock Trail from Cienaga Camp; 23.5 miles for combined ride
Time Allowed: 4 to 6 hours for total ride
Difficulty: Moderately strenuous, with technical riding
Elevation Gain: 1,000' from Cienaga Camp
Ride Type: Loop trip on fire road and trail
Road Numbers: 6N32, 6N32C
Topo Maps: Whitaker Peak, Liebre Mountain
Comments: The Redrock Loop from Cienaga Camp has numerous stream crossings, and there is water in the stream beds most of the year, although none of it is for drinking. The downhill section from the shoulder of Redrock Mountain is rough, steep, and rocky, with many tight switchbacks. Use caution! The March 1992 floods heavily eroded sections of the trail. You have to portage sections of Cienaga Canyon from Piano Box to the top. A fire in 1996 changed the vista in some places along this route, but it also probably improved the riding conditions. This ride borders on a Condor Refuge area that is closed to travel.

Located north of Castaic Lake, Cienaga Camp is a very pretty and remote campground. To reach the camp from I-5 in Castaic, take Lake Hughes Road from Castaic 11 miles north to Warm Springs Rehabilitation Center. From here, you can either drive west on 6N32 if the seasonal gate is open, or park outside the gate and ride to the camp.

To ride to Cienaga Camp from the gate at Lake Hughes Road, go west on 6N32, which climbs gradually as it winds through the oak-shaded canyon. At 0.9 mile, you reach the remains of Warm Springs Camp, which was destroyed in the 1987 Ruby Canyon fire. From Warm Springs Camp, you climb steeply in stages to a three-way junction at 2.7 miles. Ride west on the left-center road toward Cienaga Camp. (The right road heads northwest to Sawtooth Mountain, the left road toward Warm Springs Mountain). Descending in stages, you reach the camp at 7.0 miles.

Cienaga Camp once saw lots of use, but seasonal road closures from Lake Hughes Road and a permanent closure from Templin Highway are quickly isolating the area. Red Rock Mountain, northwest of the camp, is a condor sanctuary and is off limits to travel.

From Cienaga Camp, you can ride back to the start for a 14-mile outing. To continue on Redrock Trail, however, reset your computer to 0.0 mile. Go north up the road toward Fish Canyon. Cross the metal fence that prevents autos from going up Fish Canyon. Ride north, crisscrossing the oak-lined stream until you reach the end of the road at Piano Box. Now only a depression in the hillside on your right, this area was named for an actual piano box that was used as safe storage for food and supplies for the miners at Rodgers Camp, which was once located farther up the canyon.

Portage across Fish Creek to your left and begin to bike and hike up the moderately brushy shoulder of Redrock Mountain. At 2.5 miles and 960 feet higher, you come to the top of Redrock Shoulder. From here you can look west toward the Old Ridge Route, Cobblestone Mountain, and the West Sespe drainage. Continue west down the rocky side of Redrock Mountain, an 880-foot descent. The trail switchbacks very sharply and is crisscrossed by rocky stream beds.

At 4.1 miles you reach Redrock Creek after passing through several intriguing rock formations. From here, you can see the beautiful red sandstone face of Redrock Mountain to the north. Go west across the meadow, then head left and climb up to a road junction. At 4.5 miles, go left again. (The trail to the right is closed for condor research.) You now begin a very rocky descent to Castaic Creek. Use extreme caution! Control your speed and mind dangerous Redrock Canyon on your left.

At 5.3 miles, you reach the bottom and cross Redrock Creek again. Continue south down Castaic Canyon. The trail here is an old road bed that has gone back to nature. The trail crisscrosses Castaic Creek several times, but is still very fast. At 6.1 miles, the trail is washed out. Go right for 100 feet and then left to pick up the trail again. At 7.2 miles, after a small stretch of fire road, you reach Templin Highway Bridge. Go southeast on unsigned 6N32 for about 100 yards and then left up Fish Canyon to Cienaga Campground. At 8.0 miles, you come to a gate that is generally closed during winter. Continue up the narrowing canyon. In fact, the canyon is so tight that some sections of the creek have been paved to create a road. In some of the wider spots, cool pools of water with moss and ferns line the road. At 9.5 miles, you arrive back at shady Cienaga Camp. If you parked near Lake Hughes Road, return east on 6N32, adding another 7 miles to the ride for a total of 23.5 miles.

Cienaga Loop

Trip Length: 24.7 miles
Time Allowed: 5 hours
Difficulty: Strenuous, some technical sections
Elevation Gain: 1,800'
Ride Type: Loop trip on fire road and singletrack
Road Numbers: 6N32, 7N13, OHV, 6N13
Topo Maps: Whitaker Peak, Warm Springs Mountain
Comments: Recommended for experienced riders in good shape. Avoid the ride in hot weather since there is virtually no shade. Bring plenty of water with you. Best seasons are spring to fall. The ride begins the same as Warm Springs Mountain ride, but continues beyond the lookout, adding a 12-mile loop.

From I-5 in Castaic, take Lake Hughes Road north 11 miles to Warm Springs Rehabilitation Center at the beginning of 6N32. Ride west on 6N32, which climbs gradually through the oak-shaded canyon. In spring and fall the creek bubbles next to the road and there are several small crossings. At 0.9 mile you reach the graded remains of Warm Springs Camp. Past the camp the road climbs in stages.

At 2.7 miles you come to a three-way junction. Take the far left road, 7N13, up Warm Springs Mountain. The climb is sometimes steep, but not long. As you ascend, more of the Saugus backcountry can be seen: Burnt Peak with its radio towers to the north, the shoulder of Liebre Mountain in the northeast, and Sawtooth Mountain's long ridges to the northeast. To the east is Bouquet Reservoir.

At 6.0 miles you roll onto the shoulder of Warm Springs Mountain. Continue to the gate at 6.2 miles. Above you on the summit are the remains of Warm Springs Lookout Tower. Although the tower was destroyed in the 1987 Ruby Canyon fire, the small stand of pine trees there miraculously survived.

Take the road to the right of the gate and descend. Warm Springs Mountain has a shallow cup-shaped top called Necktie Basin. This grassy dell, with its small stream, was once home to Native Americans. It is a beautiful place to stop and take a break, especially in the spring when wildflowers bloom in the meadow. After a short break, continue across Necktie Basin and begin to climb the southwest slopes. The road rollercoasters and is very rocky. At 8.2 miles there is a turnout and a large cistern. From here you have a fantastic view of Castaic Lake far below you, and glimpses of things to come.

Now the fun begins! Descend southwest toward Castaic Lake on a steep, rocky fire road, using caution. This is definitely a place to improve your downhill skills. After about 2 miles of fast, sometimes brutal descending, you come to a paved road. Continue right on the pavement. The road drops quickly and then rollercoasters, sometimes steeply, to the northwest. As you ride, you pass many stands of pine with Castaic Lake nearby on your left. At 11.7 miles, stay on the road to your right and begin to climb.

After about a mile the road levels a bit and nears Elderberry Forebay, the uppermost part of Castaic Lake (the lake is divided into three sections). You can see the huge pipes here coming down from Templin Highway to the power plant at the head of the lake. At 16.1 miles you pass a gate and enter a sandy stretch that parallels Castaic Creek. Keep to your right. At 16.9 miles you reach 6N32 (unsigned) and turn right, heading up Fish Canyon. You pass a gate and the canyon narrows soon after, and in some places the road is actually the paved-over creek bed. (Be careful of slippery moss and algae.) Continue up canyon to Cienaga Campground. Oak-shaded beaches and quiet surroundings make this a perfect place to rest before the final part of the ride.

After a break, head east out of Cienaga Camp and begin climbing steeply. The road levels after a while and then climbs to the junction of 6N32 and 7N13. From here you return down 6N32 to your parking spot.

An optional return is Allegheny Trail, but it is not in good condition at this time. If you choose to ride it, be totally self-sufficient and prepared for rough travel, portages, and poison oak. Turn right on 7N13, and about 100 feet past a little hill on your left, Allegheny drops into Warm Springs Canyon. Mountain bikers worked on this trail several times in 1992 to clear trees and repair switchbacks, but floods of March 1993 and subsequent winters have again made the bottom section very difficult. We have not ridden the trail since then, and it may not be easy to follow. At first, you switchback down to the floor of Warm Springs Canyon. The trail jumps the creek many times. Tall grass and hidden round stones can make this a singletracker's delight or bane! When you reach 6N32 again, ride east down the cool, shaded canyon 0.9 mile to Lake Hughes Road and your starting point.

CHAPTER 12

Sawmill Mountain and Liebre Mountain

Upper Shake Campground and Sawmill Campground

Trip Length: 6 to 9 miles
Time Allowed: 1 to 2 hours
Difficulty: Easy to fairly strenuous
Elevation Gain: 600' to 1,300'
Ride Type: Fire road out-and-back
Road Numbers: 7N23, 7N23B
Topo Map: Burnt Peak
Comments: The variances in mileage and elevations indicate there is more than one way to skin this route—either as an easy or moderately strenuous ride. Upper Shake and Sawmill campgrounds are the loveliest in the district, and spring and fall are particularly good times to visit.

We get to this ride via I-5 to Castaic and then driving the 25 miles up Lake Hughes Road, but it is accessible from many directions (consult your map). From the intersection of Lake Hughes Road and Lake Elizabeth Road, turn left (northwest) and you immediately find yourself on Pine Canyon Road. Approximately 4.4 miles up Pine Canyon Road you can see an area on the left and a road leading into the mountains. A sign here reads *Upper Shake 3 mi., Sawmill Campground 5 mi., Burnt Peak 7 mi.* Park at this dirt area.

Jump on your bikes and begin climbing immediately up 7N23 past the sign for Upper Shake. This section is a constant uphill, but for the average rider it is an entirely manageable grade. As you continue you come to an area that gives some views of the valley to the east toward Rosamond, and as you continue to climb, you can look ahead and up toward the Sawmill and Burnt Peak areas, with their stands of oak and pine trees.

At 2.0 miles, you reach the intersection of 7N23 and 7N23B. For a nice beginner ride or simply for the adventure of it, you can take 7N23B, the upper of the two gated roads on your left, and descend into Upper Shake Campground. Upper Shake is very pretty, and it is well shaded by large pines. In summer the area is cool, while winter may bring a good covering of snow. One winter day, two of us did this route under threatening skies and found out that snow and ice have an interesting effect on mountain bike brakes. At least falling didn't hurt much! To return to 7N23, simply retrace your steps back up the fire road.

To head up to Sawmill Campground, return to 7N23, turn left, and continue up the mountain on a steeper grade. The surroundings become less and less like the usual brushy hills of the Saugus District as you ride past large pines and oaks. Several viewpoints along the way give you the opportunity to see the west end of Antelope Valley and points north.

At 3.5 miles, you reach the saddle at Burnt Peak. Here you are at a junction of three fire roads. To your right is a sign for Sawmill Campground (a mile ahead), and you ride in that direction on 7N23. Ride

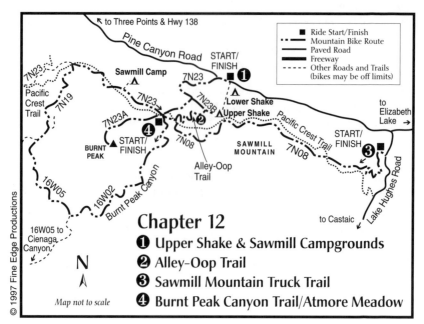

Chapter 12

❶ **Upper Shake & Sawmill Campgrounds**
❷ **Alley-Oop Trail**
❸ **Sawmill Mountain Truck Trail**
❹ **Burnt Peak Canyon Trail/Atmore Meadow**

uphill for just a little longer, as you move along into a nice, grassy grove of black oaks that turn vivid colors in the later part of the year— flaming reds, oranges and browns from nature's palette.

At 4.9 miles, after a short downhill, you reach the turn-off to Sawmill Campground. Taking off to the right, the road descends into a cool and shady picnic area with tables. Here on the north side of Sawmill Mountain at 5,200 feet, the wind is nearly a constant companion, and the sound of the pines being gently stirred by these breezes is soothing. This campground sees some use, although it has never been occupied by more than three or four campers in the times that we have been there.

Return to your vehicle by retracing your route down 7N23. It is very nearly all downhill on the return leg. It's a great downhill, too, with challenging corners and reasonably good surfaces. There are some loose, rocky sections, so use caution. Watch for vehicle traffic, since this road is an access used by many visitors.

Alley-Oop Trail
(from 7N08 to Upper Shake Campground)

Trip Length: The trail is 1 mile long, and is usually ridden as a loop option on any ride bringing you to the junction of 7N23, 7N23A, and 7N08 (such as the Upper Shake/Sawmill ride described above).
Time Allowed: Varies; 1 hour or more
Difficulty: Technical
Elevation Gain: 760'
Ride Type: Trail
Topo Map: Burnt Peak. (This ride is not shown on the USFS map, so consult the topo map for detailed study.)
Comments: This trail earns a technical rating for its narrow upper half, which is somewhat exposed and follows steep switchbacks. The bottom half is much easier and fun to ride. No brush interferes, and the half dozen or so jumps near the bottom earned this trail the name Alley-Oop.

Follow the driving and riding instructions in the previous ride to the intersection of 7N23, 7N23A, and 7N08 between Upper Shake and Sawmill campgrounds. From the intersection, go east on 7N08 for half a mile. At the first right-hand sweeper, Alley-Oop Trail dives off from a wide spot on the left and heads due east. About 25 feet down you cross the Pacific Crest Trail. It is clearly marked and easy to distinguish from the trail you are on. Do not ride on the Pacific Crest Trail; it is off limits to bicycle travel.

Continuing straight ahead and down, you pass a sign that reads *Upper Shake 1 mile, Lower Shake 2 miles.* Just past this sign is a sharp switchback to the right. Control your speed at all times, since the top section is full of these beauties, some rideable, some not. Use caution: They tend to sneak up on you. One of these is reached at 0.6 mile and is a sharp, sharp, switchback to the left. Walk your bike around. If you overshoot this one, you will run right over the edge for a very painful drop.

After the switchbacks, the trail narrows and follows along a hillside. There is a fair amount of exposure here, so watch your speed and choose your lines carefully. As you move along, the grade eases a little and the trail opens up and becomes truly a joy to ride. There is little brush to contend with, and a series of bumps in the trail discourages vehicles and makes for a high grin factor. Some of the bumps are quite high, so be very careful lest you fly more than God intended you to. At 2.0 miles, you come to the road to Upper Shake Campground, 7N23B.

This trail could be worked into many loop trips. Starting from Upper Shake, riding up 7N23, and returning on the trail would be 3 to 4 miles.

Sawmill Mountain Truck Trail with Burnt Peak Option

Trip Length: 18 to 23.5 miles
Time Allowed: 2.5 to 4 hours
Difficulty: Very strenuous; nontechnical
Elevation Gain: 2,200' to 2,700'
Ride Type: Fire road out-and-back with pavement loop option
Road Number: 7N08
Topo Maps: Lake Hughes, Burnt Peak
Comments: This is a lovely ride and shows some very nice views off the east side of Sawmill Mountain. The climb is long but never very difficult, and the return half of the ride is mostly downhill. There are several options in this ride, including a choice of return route and whether or not you want to summit Burnt Peak, the highest point in the range.

From Castaic on I-5, drive 25 miles up Lake Hughes Road. Just 0.3 mile before reaching Pine Canyon Road, 7N08 takes off to the west. Located among some houses, it would be difficult to recognize as an entrance to one of the most beautiful areas of the Saugus District if it weren't for the sign. Park your vehicle along the beginning of this road, being careful not to block access to any of the residences here. The road is in excellent condition, and it is mostly a middle chain ring ride as you work your way up the shoulder of Sawmill Mountain.

After riding up 7N08 a little over 2 miles and 800 feet of elevation gain, you pass a television antenna site. Springtime brings a carpet of wildflowers among the small pines planted here.

At 3.9 miles you come to a fork. Take the left road and descend, enjoying great views of Elizabeth Lake and the surrounding community. It is easy travelling for a while, and at 4.2 miles you pass by some beautiful black oaks. At 5.5 miles, you begin climbing again, passing some mature pines, and the view to the east is striking at times. At 7.8 miles, look left for a fantastic view of four consecutive mountain ridges all the way to the San Gabriels. Here you work a little harder, because the grade increases and the road is sandy in places.

After about 8 miles, all the uphill work is done as you roll over the shoulder of Sawmill Mountain. You have labored your way up 2,200 feet of elevation gain and can cruise downhill for a while until, at 9.8 miles and about two hours of riding, you reach an intersection with 7N23 and 7N23A (you are travelling on 7N08). To the west is Burnt Peak, with microwave towers perched atop its 5,700-foot crown.

Straight ahead lies Sawmill Campground and the road to Atmore Meadows and Liebre Mountain. To the right is 7N23, one of the return options.

Rest here if you like and enjoy the beauty of an area that is very much out of character with the rest of the Saugus Range. Instead of scrub oak and buckthorn, deciduous oaks and pines surround you. Smog? Only what is below you obscuring the valleys from view. While summer is fine for riding here (it is usually cooler at this elevation), fall is our favorite time to visit. The air is clearer and the leaves are turning. Late in the winter though, expect snow.

If you wish to visit Burnt Peak, it is a challenging but short 2.7 miles on 7N23A with 588 feet of climbing that rewards you with fairly fantastic views of the surrounding countryside. (Note that mileages to and from Burnt Peak are not combined with the ride mileages that follow.) A sign points the way at the crossroads of 7N23, 7N23A (gated) and 7N08. The electronic site crowning the mountaintop is easy to see from the starting point. Although you start by descending, the road soon climbs fairly steeply, winding around the north side of Burnt Peak before popping out on top. At 2.5 miles, take the right road. At 2.7 miles, you come to a gate. To the right, a road leads to more microwave facilities a little lower on the mountain.

It would be a shame to come this far and not go to the top, so walk the remaining 30 feet or so past the gate and up to the summit. The view speaks for itself. One clear and cold winter day, with the ground frozen beneath our feet, we could see the faint glimmer of the Pacific Ocean on the horizon.

There is nowhere to go but down, and the return trip to the saddle is a simple retrace of your path to the top.

Back at the crossroads, you have more choices. You may continue north on 7N23 and rest at Sawmill Campground (1.4 miles north from the crossroads, on the right of 7N23). Or you could turn right and head down 7N23 and enjoy a fine downhill run to Pine Canyon Road 3.1 miles farther. Turning right onto the paved Pine Canyon Road provides a fast, big-ring pavement return to Lake Hughes Road, where you would turn right and ride the short distance to your starting point.

Our favorite option is to return on the route we came up, taking 7N08 back down to Lake Hughes Road. Remember the long climb to the saddle? Going back it becomes a long downhill, the last section being a real hoot as you plunge down to your starting point.

Burnt Peak Canyon Trail/ Atmore Meadows

Trip Length: 16.2 miles
Time Allowed: 5 to 7 hours
Difficulty: Very strenuous and fairly technical
Elevation Gain: 2,500'
Ride Type: Loop ride on trail and fire road
Road Number: 16W02
Topo Map: Burnt Peak
Comments: This is a very demanding ride: a large elevation gain and loss combined with a good amount of portaging through a creek area will test your trail skills. A topo map and a compass are recommended, along with more water than you think you will use. Avoid doing this route in the heat of summer (temperatures of 120° have been recorded on the canyon floor) and *don't do this alone.*

Following the directions in the Sawmill Mountain Truck Trail ride described above, drive to the saddle on Sawmill Mountain where 7N23, 7N23B, and 7N08 join. Here, Burnt Peak Canyon Trail (16W02) is hidden from plain view. Standing at the crossroads and facing southwest toward Burnt Peak, walk south to the edge of the road and head east toward 7N08. Before you go very far, you'll find 16W02 heading downhill to the south. (You actually could begin from any point in the area and add as much difficulty as you like by riding to the crossroads. For instance, Sawmill Campground would be a good optional starting point.)

Trail 16W02 is singletrack and doubletrack for 3.5 miles, and it is a fantastic ride–challenging but not too difficult. It's steep in places and gives good break-in time for new brake pads! You descend to a creek bed as the trail continues. At 3.5 miles you climb over a small ridge on a sandy trail that is still clean and easy to follow. Caution: From this point, the trail becomes sandy, brushy, and intermittent. In addition, there is a 1,500-foot push to Atmore Meadows. If this sounds like too much for you, turn back at this point. If not, continue over the ridge and down through another creekbed, which you reach at approximately 5.2 miles. At this point the trail is intermittent at times, but continues west.

At 6 miles, you reach a split in the trail. Follow the creek northwest, taking the right-hand trail, 16W05 (there was a sign here marking the junction the last time I rode this). If you continued straight on 16W05 toward Cienaga Camp, you'd find the trail brushed over and disappearing after a while.

After turning right on 16W05, the ride changes personality. The trail is nonexistent for large portions, and much portaging and pushing is required to make headway. This is where a compass and topo map are useful. Follow the creek bed and watch for portions of trail and pieces of ribbon tied to branches marking the trail direction. This section is one reason that this is not a beginner's ride. Caution: If you are not confident in your abilities at this point, turn back now. The rest of you wear your Daniel Boone hats.

At approximately 7 miles, the trail turns north and uphill. It takes off to the right and can be difficult to locate. It is not marked. You sympathize with mountain goats as you push up 1,500 feet of switchback trail that heads toward Atmore Meadows. Continue on, bypassing the trail to Gilette Mine (16W03) to reach Atmore Meadows at 10.3 miles. This is a pretty area and makes for a good rest spot before continuing your climb out.

After recovering, head back down the road out of Atmore Meadows and follow 7N19 around and up to 7N23. Turn right (east) and work your way uphill back toward the Sawmill Camp area, seen ahead of you as a grassy, forested section. At 16.2 miles, you reach the saddle at Burnt Peak and the trailhead where you began this loop.

Liebre Mountain to Golden Eagle Trail

Trip Length: 16.2 miles
Time Allowed: 3 to 4 hours
Difficulty: The full loop is strenuous and fairly technical. The level of difficulty can be varied by shortening the loop into smaller loops or driving to the top of the mountain.
Elevation Gain: 1,500'
Ride Type: Fire road and trail loop with small pavement section
Road Number: 7N23
Topo Map: Liebre Mountain
Comments: This fairly long climb on a good fire road up the west shoulder of Liebre Mountain offers excellent views. The trail return is fun and not too difficult, with some of the finest legal singletrack in the entire range. No water.

Travel north on I-5 from Castaic and exit at the Highway 138/Quail Lake off-ramp. Drive 4.2 miles to the turnoff for the Old Ridge Route Road. Turn right. Drive uphill on 8N04, a paved road, for 2.6 miles to the ruins of Sandbergs Resort on the right. Park here. These foundations are all that's left of one of the greatest rest stops on the Old Ridge Route.

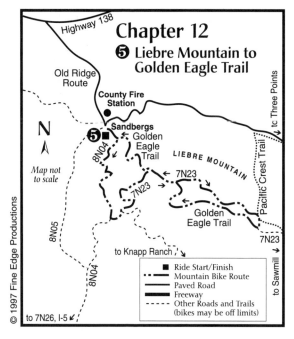

After unloading, return to the pavement of 8N04 and start riding south. Cruise along on the broken pavement until at 2.6 miles you come to Road 7N23. Turn left. The sign on the left reads *Castaic 25 mi, Bear Campground 9 mi, Sawmill Campground 14 mi.* Except for a short section near the top, the first mile on 7N23 is the steepest of the entire ride. Don't lose heart, it gets easier. At 3.2 miles, keep left, bypassing 7N22. This road heads to Knapp Ranch and is not recommended, since it goes to private property. The ranch is used for cattle and the area is fenced.

Settle in and enjoy the climb on 7N23, because the road improves considerably and the views start to come into their own. Beyond Pyramid Lake to the south are White Mountain, Black Mountain, and Cobblestone Mountain. Looking more westerly you see Hungry Valley, Frazier Mountain, and the rolling Gorman Hills.

At 6.5 miles, you reach the first summit and begin to roll along more gradually. There are too many roads branching off 7N23 to mention, but the main road is always clearly defined. The terrain becomes strikingly pretty as you move into lovely oak woodland. Keep an eye out for golden eagles soaring on the thermals above you, a reminder of the solitude the backcountry can offer. At 7.8 miles, a short, rocky climb brings you over the top. Roll along to 9.8 miles, and just after a small rise in the road, a doubletrack trail takes off to the left. You take the doubletrack, and just 0.1 mile down you come to a fence and a sign that reads *Bear Camp 2 mi, Burnt Peak Junction 10 mi, Wilderness Camp 1 mi, Oakdale Canyon Road 5 mi.* (The Pacific Crest Trail, which incorporates 17W01 from here to Horse Camp Canyon, is closed to bicycle traffic.) To pick out Golden Eagle Trail, follow the fence line to the left. At first it seems only a game path through the trees, but it soon opens to a good trail winding through the oaks.

The ride at this point is easy and runs slightly uphill. Except for some occasional brush and fallen limbs, beginners will have little trouble on this section. At 10.6 miles you cross 7N23 and pick up the trail on the other side to the southwest. The route passes through some brushy parts but is still a good, clean trail. At 11.8 miles you cross a spur road from 7N23 and continue straight across this road on a doubletrack for 300 feet or so. On the right, with a massive old oak in the background, the trail picks up again. There should be a stake with a yellow ribbon marking the trail. After a little bit, you drop into a gorgeous oak forest as the trail rollercoasters along a hillside. (Watch for little nubs of oak root sticking up out of the trail. They are hard to pick out of the shadows and could easily cause a flat.) After leaving the oak forest, the trail opens up as you roll toward a lovely grassy knoll with a great view of Pyramid Lake.

At 13.7 miles, you cross 7N23 again. From here the going becomes more difficult due to brush crowding over the trail. It seems to have been cleared somewhat in late 1996 and is now in pretty good shape. If you like, turn left on 7N23 and enjoy a fun fire road descent on 7N23 back to the Old Ridge Route. Caution: This is a long, fast descent, so control your speed at all times. To continue on the trail, cross 7N23 and follow the singletrack. At 16.2 miles, the Ridge Route Road is visible to the left. Drop down to the road, turn right and ride the last 100 feet to your vehicle.

CHAPTER 13

The Old Ridge Route and Oak Flats

The Old Ridge Route Road

Trip Length: Varies; 30 miles one way if done in its entirety
Time Allowed: Varies
Difficulty: Easy to strenuous; nontechnical
Elevation Gain: Varies
Ride Type: Out-and-back on pavement
Road Number: 8N04
Topo Maps: Liebre Mountain, Whitaker Peak, Warm Springs Mountain
Comments: The Old Ridge Route is such a long road that few people travel its full length in one trip, even though it is certainly possible to do so. Instead, excursions from one end into the middle and back out again are the norm. If you want to make the whole journey in a day, we recommend that you have someone shuttle you to the north end and that you ride south to Castaic. This is by far the easiest way to go. The upper reaches of 8N04 are remote, but they are used quite often and vehicle traffic is always a possibility.

Because there is no water available on 8N04, take ample supplies with you.

The Old Ridge Route Road, otherwise known as the Grapevine, had a relatively short but busy history. In 1909, legislation calling for better highways prompted engineers to plan a shorter route from Newhall to Gorman, bypassing the trip around Elizabeth Lake and Pine Canyon. They surveyed a road directly along a ridge top, hence the name Ridge Route. Interestingly, the name of the man to survey the route was Lewis Clark. With its completion in 1915, the new highway was hailed by the Automobile Club of Southern California as "the last word in scientific highway building."

Be that as it may, the road soon developed a reputation as a killer due to its steep grades and narrow lanes. Sharp curves bordered steep dropoffs into canyons near the edge of the roadways. Many a

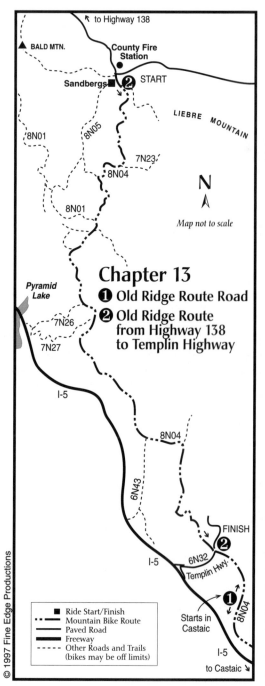

to Highway 138

▲ BALD MTN.

County Fire
Station

Sandbergs■ ❷ START

LIEBRE MOUNTAIN

8N01

8N05

7N23

8N04

N
∧

Map not to scale

8N01

Pyramid
Lake

7N26

7N27

Chapter 13
❶ Old Ridge Route Road
❷ Old Ridge Route from Highway 138 to Templin Highway

I-5

8N04

6N43

FINISH
❷
6N32
I-5
Templin Hwy

❶
8N04

Starts in
Castaic

I-5
to Castaic ↘

Legend:
■ Ride Start/Finish
▪▪▪ Mountain Bike Route
── Paved Road
━━ Freeway
--- Other Roads and Trails
(bikes may be off limits)

© 1997 Fine Edge Productions

traveller found his motorcar at the bottom of these ravines due to failed brakes or miscalculations.

Still, it was heavily travelled. To cater to the needs of weary travellers, a good many roadside rest stops and gas stations sprang up along the route–places with names like the Tumble Inn, Halfway Inn, Lebec, and the most gracious of all, Sandbergs Motor Inn. Little remains of these sites except crumbling foundations. Bypassed in 1933 by the faster and wider Highway 99 and later by I-5, the old road is seldom used today.

For mountain bikers, this is a pleasant area to ride. The Ridge Route still exists, continuous from Castaic to Highway 138 and broken only by Templin Highway. The road is maintained from Castaic to Templin Highway and can be driven by auto, but it has deteriorated greatly north of here.

If you ride from Castaic north toward Templin Highway, 8N04

is a good paved road suitable for all types of bicycles. On any given weekend you will likely encounter a number of cyclists on the road. Oh, one little thing: From Castaic to Templin Highway is 7.5 miles and 98 percent uphill. It is still not too difficult, being a good paved road and all, so don't be put off by this.

To start this section in the town of Castaic, take Lake Hughes Road off I-5 and proceed to the Fisherman's Landing parking lot on the corner of Lake Hughes Road and the Old Ridge Route Road. Ride the Old Ridge Route Road north past the west side of the lower lagoon of Castaic Lake. Continue past the workings of the Castaic Brickyard and on toward Templin Highway. For part of the time you parallel I-5. This portion of 8N04 is not as remote as the upper sections, but it is still quiet and peaceful for a paved road. At 7.5 miles you reach the intersection with Templin Highway. You can ride on as your heart and legs desire, but be advised that the road soon deteriorates past this point. The rest of the Old Ridge Route from the opposite end is described in the next ride. Oh yes, getting back to your vehicle is incredibly simple. Just turn around and enjoy a 7.5-mile downhill!

The Old Ridge Route from Highway 138 to Templin Highway

Trip Length: 26.5 miles
Time Allowed: 3 to 4 hours
Difficulty: Moderate
Elevation Loss: 2,500 feet to Castaic
Ride Type: One way on pavement
Road Number: 8N04
Topo Maps: Liebre Mountain, Whitaker Peak, Warm Springs Mountain
Comments: This shuttle ride is mostly downhill on rough pavement.

Take I-5 north from Castaic and exit at the Quail Lake/Highway 138 off-ramp. Drive 4.2 miles to the Old Ridge Route Road and turn right. You can start anywhere, but 2.6 miles farther up 8N04 is the site of the Old Sandbergs Resort—an attractive spot and a good place to park and start your ride.

Opened in 1916 by Herman Sandberg, the Sandberg Hotel and Motor Inn was styled as a grand Swiss chalet. Along with meals and lodging, rumor has it there was gambling and vice of a more feminine nature available at Sandbergs. The main building burned down in the early 1940s. By then, traffic had long since bypassed the Old Ridge

Route with the opening of Highway 99 in 1933.

Reset your computer to 0.0 at Sandbergs and ride down 8N04. The pedaling is easy on the road surface of broken asphalt. In some sections you ride on the original surface of steel reinforced concrete. At 2.7 miles, you pass the turn-off for 7N23. Continue on 8N04, still easy going. After 500 feet or so, a road to the right takes you to what is shown on the topo map as the Tumble Inn Campground, although there are no facilities. At 3.9 miles you come to the ruins of the Tumble Inn, another one of the rest stops along the Old Ridge Route. Here there is a sign indicating that it is 5 miles to Reservoir Summit and 23 miles to Castaic. Here also the south end of 8N05 heads down into Liebre Gulch.

Continue down 8N04, and at 5.3 miles you pass 8N01 on your right. At 6.2 miles, just before you pass under the high voltage lines that cross 8N04, the turn-out on the left is the site of the Halfway Inn, yet another one of the rest stops that sprang up along the road to meet the needs of weary travellers. Nothing remains of this one except scattered bits of broken glass and china.

You descend for a short time before beginning the climb to Reservoir Summit, one of the highest points on the Ridge Route. The climb is not very difficult and 8.4 miles finds you at the summit. Road 7N27 heads up to a small plateau and a stand of pines. There was a

lookout station here at one time, but now there is only the wind through the pines. (Road 7N26 takes off near here and drops steeply into Posey Canyon heading toward Pyramid Lake.) Reservoir Summit makes a great lunch stop, with good views of Liebre Mountain, Red Rock Mountain, and Warm Springs Mountain. This is a good spot to turn around and ride the easy 8.4 miles back to your vehicle at Sandbergs.

If you continue ahead to meet a shuttle, it is mostly downhill to Templin Highway. At 13.7 miles you come to the final set of ruins. This was the Hiway Inn, and the steps and partial foundation are located on your right under the ever-present power lines. After 19 miles of cranking you reach Templin Highway. Castaic is 7.5 miles farther south on the same route.

Townsend Peak

Trip Length: 6.5 miles
Time Allowed: 1 hour
Difficulty: Fairly strenuous; nontechnical
Elevation Gain: 400'
Ride Type: Fire road out-and-back
Road Number: 6N38
Topo Map: Whitaker Peak
Comments: Not too long or difficult, this ride gives you a glimpse of the Piru backcountry. Along with the Whitaker Peak and Oak Flats rides below, it marks the westernmost boundary of the Angeles National Forest at the edge of Los Padres National Forest. Pyramid Lake offers fishing and watersports. Piru Creek, which runs out of the base of Pyramid Dam, is stocked with trout. On any given weekend, the creek will be lined with fishermen trying their luck. These three rides also contain a remaining section of the old Golden State Highway, or "Old 99." Opened in 1934, it was replaced in 1970 by Interstate 5 and now serves only as access to some ranches and this portion of National Forest. Please note that there is no water available in this area.

On I-5, heading north from Castaic, exit at Templin Highway. Go left at the stop sign and cross under the freeway. Turn left on Golden State Highway and proceed to the road's southern end. Begin the ride here. You can see 6N38 heading south and uphill.

The first 0.4 mile is steep—steeper than the rest of the ride. But don't worry, it gets easier. At about 0.7 mile, Whitaker Peak comes into view to the northwest with rugged and steep Canton Canyon below. At 1.6 miles, bear right at a fork. You descend for a half mile or so, but quickly regain all the elevation you lost. Rolling along easier now, you reach the road's end at 3.2 miles.

Looking to the west, once again Whitaker Peak is clearly seen with the electronic site visible below the actual 4,148-foot summit. Looking a little more westward and behind Whitaker Peak is Cobblestone Mountain. Not visible, but due south, is Lake Piru. In between are views of the rugged boundary of the Angeles and Los Padres National Forests.

This spot is also the trailhead of 17W05, the Devils Canyon trail. This is an unmaintained singletrack, and is very brushy in parts with some very technical sections. Since it is mostly in Los Padres National Forest and also crosses private property, it will not be described in detail in this book.

To return to your vehicle, simply head back the way you came. The return portion of the ride is the easy part—downhill with the exception of two short climbs. It gets steep at the bottom and sees a fair amount of use by vehicles, so use common sense on the way down.

Whitaker Peak

Trip Length: 9 miles
Time Allowed: 90 minutes
Difficulty: Strenuous but nontechnical
Elevation Gain: 1,200'
Ride Type: Fire road out-and-back with loop alternate
Road Number: 6N53
Topo Map: Whitaker Peak
Comments: Once the site of a USFS lookout station, Whitaker Peak is not too difficult to reach. The first 2 miles are steep but paved, and the top gives some fine views of the country behind Piru Lake. *Note:* This may someday become a gated road, so check with the Forest Service before riding.

From I-5 in Castaic, go north and exit at Templin Highway, then turn left, and pass under the freeway. Turn right on the old Golden State Highway and continue about 2 miles to Road 6N53. Park here. Begin riding up 6N53, which is marked by a sign on the left side of the highway that reads *Whitaker Peak Rd. 6N53, Whitaker Peak 4.5 miles.* It is a paved ribbon winding its way up from your starting place. At about 1.1 miles, stay right and continue climbing on the pavement. Keep left at 2.0 miles, again staying on pavement. The road here, although still a good asphalt surface, is partially covered with sand and gravel. This is downhill for a half mile and is quite steep. Sand-covered pavement makes for poor traction, and most of the sand seems to lurk in blind corners. Control your speed.

After reaching the bottom of the pavement, you begin the final climb to Whitaker Peak. The rest of the journey is on dirt. At 2.8 miles and a sharp bend in the road, look to your right across Ruby Canyon to see some interesting rock formations. Also, looking west, you can clearly see Cobblestone Mountain. As you near the 3-mile point, you can look up and see the microwave towers on Whitaker Peak. Approaching the top, keep to the right road and bypass the fenced area around the towers. (The right path takes you to the site of the old lookout tower, now only some concrete remnants scattered through the brush. The tower was disassembled and moved to Slide Mountain in 1970.)

While the actual top of Whitaker Peak is to the north behind the microwave towers, the view from here at 4,120 feet is satisfying. To the south, you are looking down to Canton Canyon and Piru Creek as it flows into Piru Lake. Farther south are the Santa Susanna Mountains, dotted with oaks. To the east lie the San Gabriel Mountains with Mt. Wilson distinct in their midst. Looking west you can see Cobblestone and its rugged eastern drainages, while a northward view reveals Burnt Peak and Liebre Mountain. Between Cobblestone and I-5, you can see Slide Mountain with its lookout tower on top.

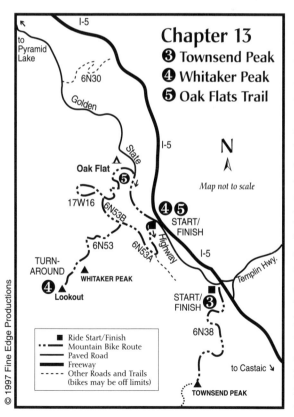

To return to your vehicle, simply retrace your route. Use caution on the trip down. The communication sites on the mountain bring vehicles this way quite frequently. There is a optional return loop through Oak Flats Campground area (see next ride).

Oak Flats Trail

Trip Length: 4.7 miles
Time Allowed: 90 minutes
Difficulty: Fairly strenuous with very technical trail sections
Elevation Gain: 800'
Ride Type: Loop trip on fire road and trail with a short pavement return
Road Numbers: 6N53, 6N53B, 17W16
Topo Map: Whitaker Peak
Comments: This ride throws sections of very demanding trail at you in spots. Most of it is quite enjoyable and not difficult, but there are several deteriorating switchbacks and eroded areas that can be hazardous. Use common sense and walk your bike through these parts. The lower section of the ride includes a posted nature trail with several types of plants highlighted for your information. The Forest Service asks that you check conditions with them before you ride 6N53B.

Follow driving directions in the preceding Whitaker Peak ride and begin cycling up 6N53. At the 2-mile point, where 6N53 drops down-hill to continue toward Whitaker Peak, there is a gated road on the right. This road, 6N53B, is closed to motor vehicles. Carry your bike around the gate on the left side. Caution: The right side of the gate has a very steep drop-off, so go around the left side.

Reset your computers to 0.0 and continue. At 0.5 mile you ride through the rock formations that are visible on the trip up to Whitaker Peak (see previous ride). At 0.9 mile, an unmarked trail takes off to your right and drops steeply down and out of sight. This is 17W16 to Oak Flats.

If you wish, there is a nice loop past the trailhead that takes you out to good views of Pyramid Lake. To do this, just continue on 6N53B, a seldom-travelled road that goes nowhere but has a fine time doing it. Continue around on the road, climbing up over a short hill as you head back in the direction you came. After a little way (the loop is only 1.3 miles long) you drop abruptly down on 6N53B to the beginning of 17W16.

Reset your computers to 0.0 at the unmarked trailhead. Trail 17W16 starts off very steep and narrow, right away telling you what you're in for. At 0.2 mile down the trail, there is a bench under an oak tree on the left, a nice spot to rest before continuing on. After a while, the trail opens up and is less demanding. As you progress, you can see posts alongside the trail counting down the mileage to Oak Flats. At 0.5 mile, there is a picnic bench under an oak overlooking the Oak Flats area. Nearing the bottom, you see plaques telling about some of the native plants found alongside the trail. These are signed as the Art Barton Nature Trail by the Rotary Club of Glendale. They add a nice touch, but are in need of refurbishing. Near the bottom you encounter a rotted out series of steps at the entrance to a switchback. Use caution and carry your bike past these steps.

At 1.3 miles, you come to Camp Verdugo Oaks, a Boy Scout camp. (Do not go into the Boy Scout Camp—it is private property.) Leave this area by continuing down past the gate to the gravelled road and turning right. Riding past Oak Flats Ranger Station, then Oak Flats Campground, you reach Golden State Highway at 1.7 miles. Turn right and follow the pavement to your vehicle where the trip ends at 2.7 miles, or 4.7 as the total loop mileage.

Chapter 14 – Mt. Pinos

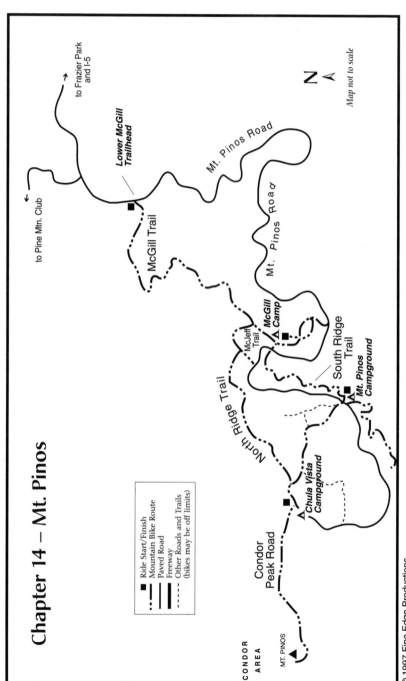

to Frazier Park
and I-5

to Pine Mtn. Club

*Lower McGill
Trailhead*

Mt. Pinos Road

Mt. Pinos Road

McGill Trail

McJeff
Trail

*McGill
Camp*

South Ridge
Trail

*Mt. Pinos
Campground*

North Ridge Trail

*Chula Vista
Campground*

Condor
Peak Road

CONDOR
AREA

MT. PINOS

N

Map not to scale

Ride Start/Finish
Mountain Bike Route
Paved Road
Freeway
Other Roads and Trails
(bikes may be off limits)

CHAPTER 14

🚲

Mt. Pinos

Mt. Pinos, the tallest peak in the small White Mountain Coastal Range, is quickly becoming one of the premiere mountain bike areas in Southern California. Located midway between Los Angeles, Lancaster, and Bakersfield, its pine-covered slopes, cool summer temperatures, and magnificent vistas beckon to the urban cyclist.

Mt. Pinos has an excellent network of hiking and crosscountry ski trails to challenge cyclists of all abilities. The McGill, Mt. Pinos, and Chula Vista camps can be used for parking to ride a favorite trail or as base camps for a weekend of exploration. There are 109 campsites with piped water and restroom facilities, all providing easy access to riding trails. Weekends are usually uncrowded, but visitors should arrive early on holidays to get a campsite. The nearby communities of Frazier Park, Pine Mt. Club, and Lake of the Woods can provide food and camping supplies. Mt. Pinos receives heavy snow in late fall and winter, so visitors should plan trips from late April to late November.

Much of Mt. Pinos is included in the new Chumash Wilderness, which was created in 1992 to keep the area unspoiled for future generations. Visitors can ride from the Chula Vista parking lot to Condor Peak Summit, but should return the same way since all trails from the summit enter Wilderness, where mountain bikes are prohibited. Another point of interest to visitors is the reintroduction of the California condor to the area. These magnificent birds lived for centuries in the Sespe Wilderness area visible to the south of Mt. Pinos. Extremely endangered, all California condors were captured and put into a breeding program to prevent total extinction. The program was successful, and the condors are now being reintroduced to the area.

The trails on Mt. Pinos are mostly short, pleasant loops in forested terrain. They are popular with hikers and equestrians, so please control your speed and use courtesy toward other visitors.

Getting There: From Interstate 5, exit at Frazier Park and head west (left) on Frazier Park Mountain Highway. A few miles after passing the Lockwood Valley turnoff, turn left on Mt. Pinos Road. McGill Campground is the first of several camping areas here. The rides in this chapter start from various campgrounds, which are shown on the Chapter 14 map.

Iris Point Trail

Trip Length: 2.2 miles
Time Allowed: 30 minutes
Difficulty: Easy
Elevation Gain: 150'
Ride Type: Trail out-and-back
Topo Map: Cuddy Valley
Comment: Great views!

From the parking lot above Mt. Pinos Camp, ride to the right on Iris Point Trail. The trail is nearly flat for most of its one-mile length. As

you ride, look to your left at the grand views of Frazier, Alamo, and Pine Mountains. The grassy meadows of Lockwood and Cuddy valleys can be seen lapping at the foot of the mountain. On a clear day, the imposing cliffs of the Topa Topas can be seen in the distance. At 0.9 mile, the trail climbs to a junction. The road to the right simply makes a loop and rejoins itself. Go left 0.1 mile to Iris Point for a clearer view of the surrounding area. Return the same way you rode in.

Knoll Loop

Trip Length: 1.5 miles
Time Allowed: 15 minutes
Difficulty: Easy
Elevation Gain: 100'
Ride Type: Loop, trail, and pavement mix
Topo Map: Cuddy Valley
Comment: This is one of the best trails for beginners.

From the north end of the Chula Vista parking lot, ride east 0.2 mile on a wide trail. To your left is Chula Vista Meadow and Chula Vista Camp. Go right at the Knoll Loop sign. The trail is wide and rolls slightly. Take your time and enjoy the surrounding pine forest. At 0.9 mile, you come back to Mt. Pinos Road. Go right, back up the pavement for an easy half-mile climb to the Chula Vista parking lot.

Harvest Trail

Trip Length: Varies; 3+ miles
Time Allowed: 45 minutes to an hour
Difficulty: Moderate
Elevation Gain: 650'
Ride Type: Trail with paved loop return
Topo Map: Cuddy Valley
Comments: This is a very enjoyable trail with some rutted sections to keep you alert.

From Chula Vista parking lot, ride 0.2 mile east to the Chula Vista Camp. The Knoll Loop trail branches off to the right. Continue straight (east), heading downhill. A small gully follows and crisscrosses the trail for most of its length. Rocks and an occasional small ditch keep you on your toes. At 1.0 mile Fir Ridge Road intersects the trail. You can go left here on Fir Ridge Road and ride 0.8 mile to a turnaround and then return to the trail, or you can go right 0.2 mile farther to Mt. Pinos Road. Mt. Pinos Camp can be seen to your left 0.2 mile down Mt. Pinos Road. If you elect not to ride back up the Harvest Trail, you can ride up Mt. Pinos Road 1.7 miles to the Chula Vista parking lot.

McJeff Trail Warm-Up

Trip Length: 1.4 miles
Time Allowed: 30 minutes
Difficulty: Moderate
Elevation: Start/end 7,429'; 151' gain/loss; high point 7,580'
Ride Type: Trail, pavement, and skid road
Season: Late April to November
Topo Map: Cuddy Valley
Comments: This is a good warm-up ride for the McGill Trail. A nice short ride in itself, it can help you get in tune with the quiet tranquility of the mountain.

Park in the McGill day use area to the right of McGill Campground. The McGill trailhead is located to the left of the campground entrance. Ride up (northwest) the McGill Trail, climbing gradually to the junction at 0.2 mile. Turn left (northwest) on Skater Trail to reach Mt. Pinos Road at 0.4 mile. Turn right, climbing on pavement to unmarked Jeffrey Pine Flat road on your right at 0.6 mile. Take that to a junction at 0.7 mile. Turn right (east) on the McJeff Trail, marked by a small jump. Ride down McJeff, using caution on the large jumps. (You may wish to ride around some of these.) Continue to the McGill/Skater Junction at 1.1 miles. Take the center left trail (McGill Trail) to return to McGill Camp at 1.4 miles.

McGill Trail

Trip Length: 8.3 miles
Time Allowed: 2 to 3 hours
Difficulty: Moderately technical, strenuous if ridden as a loop
Elevation: Start/high point 7,429'; low point 6,203'; 1,226' loss/gain
Ride Type: Trail with pavement loop return; can also be done as a shuttle, or rider can return up the trail
Season: Late April to November
Topo Map: Cuddy Valley
Comments: This excellent trail can be ridden by itself as a loop or combined with the North or South Ridge trails to link the mountain from top to bottom. This trail is also popular with hikers and equestrians, so please control your speed and use proper mountain biking trail etiquette.

Park in the McGill day use lot to the right of the McGill Campground entrance. The McGill trailhead is left of the main entrance. The sign at the trailhead shows the Whitehorn Nature Trail and the McGill Trail. The Whitehorn Nature Trail is for handicapped use only; no bikes.

Sign reads *McGill 3¾ miles to Mt. Pinos Road* (at the bottom of mountain).

Ride up the McGill trail, climbing gradually. At 0.2 mile you reach a junction. Take the trail to the right (northeast). As you ride, you can see paved Whitehorn Trail to your right downslope. At 0.3 mile, you come to another trail junction and sign. The sign indicates McGill Trail to the left and Whitehorn Trail to the right. Go left, down the McGill Trail.

The trail is a very clean singletrack, gradually falling through the pines and whitehorn. Slow at 0.8 mile to look at Frazier and Alamo Mountains to the east and the far walls of the Topatopa Mountains to the south. Continue descending, dodging the occasional patch of rocks or lone roots. To the northeast, Antelope Valley can be seen at 1.3 miles. Below on your right at 1.6 miles, you can see Cuddy Valley and regions beyond the Tehachapi Mountains looming past Tecuyah Mountain.

Resume your descent to the base of Mt. Pinos. The singletrack is exceptional; it is clean for the most part, although stones, small thickets and the odd fallen tree will keep riders from sightseeing too much. The trail to several private camps appears on your left at 2.5 miles. Please stay to the right. The trail descends steeply after this. Beware of other trail users. Here oaks begin to appear more frequently as you descend the last stretch to reach Mt. Pinos Road at 3.6 miles.

You now have several options to return to McGill Camp: 1) If you previously arranged a shuttle, jump in the car and motor back. 2) You can cycle up the pavement, a moderately strenuous climb to reach McGill Camp. 3) You can do what many local riders do and ride back up the trail. This can be strenuous and is steep at the bottom.

The reward is more singletrack and a shorter round trip of 7.2 miles. Any way you return, you'll want to ride this trail again.

South Ridge

Trip Length: 2.7 miles
Time Allowed: 45 minutes
Difficulty: Easy to mildly technical
Elevation: Start/high point 7,800'; low point 7,509'; 291' loss/gain
Ride Type: Trail, with a pavement loop return
Season: Late April to November
Topo Map: Cuddy Valley
Comments: Probably one of the most popular trails on the mountain, South Ridge is close to the Mt. Pinos and McGill campgrounds. The many small water crossings and crosscountry ski jumps will excite riders who are looking for beauty, challenge, and time to enjoy camp life.

Park just outside Mt. Pinos Campground, about 2.5 miles up the road from McGill Camp. Ride into the camp and go left at the crosscountry ski trail sign. The trail is a fairly wide crosscountry route with numerous jumps of different sizes. Small spring seepages cross the trail as you descend. The trail forks at 1.7 miles. Go left (the right trail dwindles to nothing) and at 2.0 miles you return to Mt. Pinos Road. Turn left again and ride up the pavement 0.7 mile to Mt. Pinos Camp.

North Ridge/McGill Trail

Trip Length: 5.9 miles one way, 13.9 miles round trip
Time Allowed: An hour one way; 3 hours round trip
Difficulty: Moderate to strenuous—includes jumps and a long return
Elevation: Start/high point 8,360'; low point 6,203'; 2,157' loss/gain
Ride Type: Trail, fire road, pavement return (shuttle or loop)
Season: Late April to November
Topo Map: Cuddy Valley
Comments: This is one of two routes from the end of the Mt. Pinos Road at Chula Vista Camp to the bottom of the mountain. Although not as well known as the Harvest/South Ridge Trail descent, the dense pine forest and distance from the highway and campgrounds create a more tranquil and unique experience. You can also do it as a one-way shuttle.

Park at the Chula Vista parking lot near the summit of Mt. Pinos. If you do this as a shuttle, leave a vehicle at the McGill Trailhead at the bottom of the mountain.

Ride up the Condor Peak Road 0.1 mile to a gate. Go past the gate 50 feet and take the old road to your right. This is North Ridge

Trail. A sign at 0.2 mile marks Meadow Trail to the left. Continue north-east on North Ridge Trail, straight ahead. It is wide and descends gradually. The trail becomes a singletrack at 0.8 mile and descends steeply down a rocky gully. Use necessary caution here. You reach a junction at 1.0 mile. Stay to the right on the singletrack. The trail drops left to join a Jeffrey Pine Flat (JPF) road at 1.2 miles.

Follow this JPF road east, dropping again. Roots and occasional water bars make great jumps. Ride to the junction at 2.0 miles and go left onto the McJeff Trail. The start of this is marked by a small jump. McJeff is liberally dotted with large jumps, so exercise restraint. At 2.5 miles, turn left (north) onto the unmarked McGill Trail. Continue to ride north on McGill to the junction with the Whitehorn Nature Trail at 2.6 miles. Turn left again on the McGill Trail.

Please use caution and control your speed, since this trail is heavily used by hikers and equestrians. McGill Trail drops down the lower slopes to the bottom of Mt. Pinos. On the trip down, you encounter switchbacks, occasional rocks, whitehorn booby traps, and even a fallen tree with a narrow opening cut in it. Have fun, but be careful. You reach Mt. Pinos Road at 5.9 miles.

If you left a car at the bottom, you can shuttle back up to Chula Vista Campground. Otherwise, ride the 8 miles up Mt. Pinos Road to return.

Condor Peak Road

Trip Length: 3 miles
Time Allowed: 1 hour
Difficulty: Moderate, strenuous
Elevation: High point 8,831'; low point/start 8,360'; 471' gain/loss
Ride Type: Fire road out-and-back
Season: Late April to November
Topo Maps: Sawmill Mountain, Cuddy Valley
Comments: This is a relatively rugged, though short, fire road climb to the summit of Mt. Pinos. The view from the summit is well worth the effort, and for an added bonus you can occasionally spot a condor. Please note that all trails from the summit enter wilderness (no bicycles allowed), so you must return the way you came.

Park at the Chula Vista Camp parking lot (see directions for the previous ride).

The road leaves the parking lot near its entrance on the left (west) side. At first the road is fairly smooth and the climbing relatively easy, but soon it steepens and becomes rocky. At 0.9 mile you cross a small meadow and the going becomes easier. Three small spurs join the main road: one at 0.9 mile, another at 1.2 miles, and the last at 1.4 miles. Each short spur ends at a vista point. If you explore any of the spurs, return to the main road the way you came.

Continue up the main road, passing a microwave facility on your right at 1.4 miles, and you reach the summit lookout at 1.5 miles. There are several benches here where you can relax and take in the magnificent view. To the north, San Joaquin Valley stretches out to the horizon, and the city of Bakersfield can be discerned at the south end of the valley. To the northeast, if the air is clear, the southern ramparts of the Sierra Nevada can be seen. Toward the east, Antelope Valley and the high desert stretch to the horizon. In springtime the desert explodes with color as the California poppies come into bloom. The rugged Dick Smith and Sespe Wilderness Areas stretch from west to south. These areas are home to the recently reintroduced California condor. These rare and majestic birds are sometimes spotted soaring over Mt. Pinos in their search for food.

Enjoy the view, and when you are ready, return to Chula Vista parking lot the way you came.

APPENDIX

IMBA Rules of the Trail©

The International Mountain Bicycling Association's Rules of the Trail have been recognized by the U.S. Forest Service, Bureau of Land Management, the Sierra Club, and the International Cycling Union—the world governing body of bicycle racing. These rules apply wherever you ride, including ski areas.

1. Ride on open trails only. Respect trail and road closures (ask if not sure), avoid possible trespass on private land, obtain permits and authorization as may be required. Federal and State wilderness areas are closed to cycling. Additional trails may be closed because of sensitive environmental concerns or conflicts with other users. Your riding example will determine what is closed to all cyclists!

2. Leave no trace. Be sensitive to the dirt beneath you. Even on open trails, you should not ride under conditions where you will leave evidence of your passing, such as on certain soils shortly after a rain. Observe the different types of soils and trail construction; practice low-impact cycling. This also means staying on the trail and not creating any new ones. Be sure to pack out at least as much as you pack in.

3. Control your bicycle! Inattention for even a second can cause disaster. Excessive speed maims and threatens people; there is no excuse for it!

4. Always yield trail. Make known your approach well in advance. A friendly greeting or bell is considerate and works well; startling someone may cause loss of trail access. Show your respect when passing others by slowing or even stopping. Anticipate that other trail users may be around corners or in blind spots.

5. Never spook animals. All animals are startled by an unannounced approach, a sudden movement, or a loud noise. This can be dangerous for you, others, and the animals. Give animals extra room and time to adjust to you. In passing, use special care and follow the directions of horseback riders (ask if uncertain). Running cattle and disturbing wild animals is a serious offense. Leave gates as you found them or as marked.

6. Plan ahead. Know your equipment, your ability, and the area in which you are riding, and prepare accordingly. Be self-sufficient at all times, keep your machine in good repair, and carry necessary supplies for changes in weather or other conditions. A well-executed trip is a satisfaction to you and not a burden or offense to others. Keep trails open by setting an example of responsible cycling for all mountain bicyclists.

Rules of the Trail ©1988 by International Mountain Bicycling Association (IMBA) may be used for public education purposes with the following credit given:

Dedicated to the appreciation of and access to recreational lands, non-profit IMBA welcomes your support. IMBA is a non-profit advocacy organization that promotes mountain biking that is environmentally sound and socially responsible. IMBA educates mountain bikers, helps government officials promote the sport through innovative management techniques, sets a positive image for off-road cycling, promotes volunteer trail work, and keeps trails open and in good condition for everyone. To join IMBA or receive additional information, call 303/545-9011 or write IMBA, P.O. Box 7578, Boulder, CO 80306.

The Care and Feeding of a Mountain Bike
BY R. W. MISKIMINS

ROUTINE CHECKUPS FOR YOUR BICYCLE

The key to years of fun and fitness from your mountain bike is giving it checkups on a regular basis. You need to know how to clean it, lubricate a few places, make simple adjustments, and recognize when something needs expert attention. For the average rider, most bike shops recommend tuneups once a year and complete overhauls every two to three years. All of the maintenance in between your trips to the bike shop you can do yourself. Given below is a nine-step checkup procedure–a list to run through after every extensive ride–before you head back out into the hills again.

1. CLEANUP
Unless the frame is really filthy, use a soft rag and a non-corrosive wax/polish such as Pledge to wipe off the grime and bring the old shine back. If you need to use water or soap and water prior to the polish, don't high-pressure spray directly at any of the bearing areas (pedals, hubs, bottom bracket or head set). You should clean all your components, too (including the chain and the rear cogs), but use a different rag and a lubricant such as Tri-Flow or Finish Line for wiping them down. Do not use polish or lubricants to clean your rims–an oily film will reduce your braking ability. Instead, wipe off the rims with a clean dry rag. If you need to remove rubber deposits from the sidewalls of the rims use acetone as a solvent.

2. INSPECTION
After you get the grit and grime off, check out the frame very carefully, looking for bulges or cracks. If there are chips or scratches that expose bare metal (especially when the metal is steel), use automotive or bicycle touch-up paint to cover them up. Your inspection should also include the components. Look for broken, bent or otherwise visibly damaged parts. Pay special attention to the wheels. When you spin them, watch the rim where it passes the brake pads. Look for wobbles and hops, and if there is a lot of movement, the wheel needs to be trued at home (or take it to a bike shop) before using it. Look for loose or broken spokes. And finally, carefully check your tires for sidewall damage, heavy tread wear, cuts and bulges, glass and nails, thorns, or whatever.

3. BRAKES
Grab the brakes and make sure they don't feel mushy and that the pads

are contacting the rim firmly (be certain the brake pads do not rub against the tires!). If the brakes don't feel firm, there are barrel adjusters at one or both ends of the wire cables that control the brakes—turn them counter-clockwise to take up some of the slack. If you are unsure as to the depend-ability of your brakes, for safety's sake let a bike shop check them.

4. BEARING AREAS
Most cyclists depend upon professional mechanics to fix any problems in the pedals, hubs, bottom bracket or head set, but they should be able to recognize when something is wrong. Spin the wheels, spin the crankarms (and the pedals) and move the handlebars from side to side. If you feel notches or grittiness, or if you hear snapping, grating or clicking noises, you have a problem. Check to make sure each of the four areas is prop-erly tightened. To check for looseness, try to wiggle a crankarm side to side or try to move a wheel side to side. Check your headset adjustment by holding the front brake, rocking the bike forward and backward, and listening for clunking sounds.

5. SHIFTING
Presuming your bike has gears, check to make sure you can use all of them. The most common problem is the stretching of the inner wire that operates the rear derailleur. If your bike is not shifting properly, try turn-ing the barrel adjuster, located where the cable comes out of the derailleur. Turn it just a little; usually a counterclockwise direction is what you need. Unless you know what you are doing, avoid turning the little adjustment screws on the derailleurs.

6. NUTS AND BOLTS
Make sure the nuts and bolts which hold everything together are tight. The handlebars and stem should not move around under pressure, and neither should your saddle. And make certain that the axle nuts or quick-releases that hold your wheels are fully secure—when a wheel falls off, the result is almost always crashtime. If you have quick-release hubs, they operate as follows: Mostly tighten them by holding the nut and winding the lever, but finish the job by swinging the lever over like a clamp (it's spring-loaded). Do not wind them up super tight as you would with a wingnut—for safe operation they must be clamped, and clamped very securely, with considerable spring tension! If you are at all uncertain re-garding the use of quick-releases, go by a bike shop and ask for a demon-stration.

7. ACCESSORIES
Make sure all your accessories, from water bottles to bags to pumps to lights, are operational and secure. Systematically check them all out and if

you carry flat-fixing or other on-the-road repair materials or tools, make sure you've got what you need and you know how to use what you carry. Statistics show that over 90% of all bicycle breakdowns are the result of flat tires, so it is recommended that you carry a pump, a spare tube, a patch kit, and a couple of tire levers with you whenever you ride.

8. LUBRICATION

The key to long-term mechanical happiness for you and your bike is proper and frequent lubrication. The most important area of lubrication is the chain—spray it with a Teflon-based or other synthetic oil (WD-40, household oil, and motor oil are not recommended), then wipe off all the excess. You can use the same lubricant for very sparsely coating the moving parts of your brakes and derailleurs.

9. INFLATION

You now are ready for the last step. Improper inflation can lead to blow-outs or pinch flats. Read the side of your tires to see what the recommended pressure is and fill them up. If there is a range of pressures given, use the high figure for street cycling, the low figure or near it for off-road riding.

After going through these nine steps of getting your bike ready you've earned another good long ride!

Basic Skills for Mountain Biking
BY R. W. MISKIMINS

Everybody knows how to ride a bike—at least almost everybody can ride around the neighborhood. But with the advent of the mountain bike, riding a two-wheel pedal-powered machine has gotten more complicated. Watch a pro-level mountain bike race and the need for "technical skills" will become obvious. Can you handle steep hills, big rocks, creeks, muddy bogs, loose sand, big tree roots, deep gravel, or radical washboards? These are the kinds of factors that differentiate mountain biking from road riding and that demand skills and balance above and beyond those required to ride around the neighborhood. The key to acquiring these abilities is practice—start easy and work diligently until you achieve high-level control of your bike.

1. BICYCLE
All mountain bikes are not created equal. Some are better suited to staying on pavement. They have too much weight, too long a wheelbase, ineffective braking systems, sloppy shifting, too smooth tread on the tires, poorly welded frames, and so on. As a general rule, the mountain bicycles marketed by the discount store chains, department stores, and sporting goods stores are only suited to on-road, non-abusive use. Bicycles from bike stores, excepting their least expensive models, are generally suited to heavy duty, skilled off-road use. They should be relatively light (under 30 pounds), and have a fairly short wheelbase and chainstay (for agility), moderately steep head angle (again for agility), strong and dependable braking and shifting systems, well-made frames, and knobby/aggressive tires.

For details on choosing the right bike for you, consult the experts at your local bike shop. They can help you not only with selecting a bicycle, but also with various accessory decisions, in such areas as suspension forks, bar ends, and gear ratio changes. And of extreme importance, whatever bike you decide on, get the right size for you. If a bike is too big for your height and weight, no matter how hard you try, you will never be able to properly handle it. If you are in doubt or in between sizes, for serious off-road riding opt for the smaller bike.

2. FUNDAMENTAL PRINCIPLES
There are some very general rules for off-road riding that apply all the time. The first, "ride in control," is fundamental to everything else. Balance is the key to keeping a bike upright—when you get out of control you will

lose your ability to balance the bike (that is, you'll crash). Control is directly related to speed, and excessive speed for the conditions you are facing is the precursor to loss of control. When in doubt, slow down!

The second principle for off-road riding is "read the trail ahead." In order to have time to react to changes in the trail surface and to obstacles, you should be looking ahead 10 to 15 feet. Especially as your speed increases, you want to avoid being surprised by hazardous trail features (rocks, logs, roots, ruts, and so on)—if you see them well ahead, you can pick a line to miss them, slow down to negotiate them, or even stop to walk over or around them.

The third principle is to "stay easy on the grips." One of the most common reactions by novices in tough terrain is to severely tense up, most noticeably in a "death grip" on the handlebars. This level of tightness not only leads to hand, arm and shoulder discomfort but interferes with fluid, supple handling of the bike. Grip loosely and bend at the elbows a bit—don't fight the bicycle, work with it!

The last general principle to be presented here is "plan your shifting." If you are looking ahead on the trail, there should be no shifting surprises. Anticipate hills, especially steep ascents, and shift before your drive-train comes under a strong load. Mountain bikes have a lot of gears and their proper use will make any excursion more enjoyable.

3. CLIMBING

Mountain bikes were originally single-speed, balloon-tire cruisers taken by truck or car to the top of a hill and then used for exciting and rapid descent. After a few years, they were given gears to eliminate the shuttle. Today's off-road bikes have 18 to 24 speeds, with a few extremely low gears so they can climb very steep hills. One of the keys to long or difficult climbs is attitude; it's a mental thing. You need to be able to accept an extended, aerobic challenge with the thoughts "I can do it" and, above all, "This is fun."

Your bike is made with hill-climbing in mind. Find a gear and a pace that is tolerable (not anaerobic) and try to maintain it. Pick a line ahead, stay relaxed, and anticipate shifting, as noted earlier. In addition, be alert to problems in weight distribution that occur when climbing. It is best to stay seated, keeping your weight solidly over the traction (rear) wheel if possible. However, if the slope is so steep that the front wheel lifts off of the ground, you will have to lean forward and slide toward the front of the saddle. Constant attention to weight distribution will give you optimum traction and balance for a climb. And make sure your saddle height is positioned so when your foot is at the bottom of a pedal stroke, your knee is very slightly bent—a saddle too low or too high will significantly reduce both power and control on a steep and difficult climb.

4. DESCENDING

This is where most serious accidents occur, primarily because a downhill lends itself to high speed. It is unquestionably the most exciting part of mountain bike riding—expert riders reach speeds up to 60 mph! For descents, the "stay in control" and "read the trail ahead" principles can be injury-saving. Know your ability and don't exceed it. And be certain your brakes are in good working order—don't believe the slogan "brakes are for sissies." On steep and difficult downhills everyone has to use them. Regarding braking, always apply the rear brake before the front (to avoid an "endo"—that is, flying over the handlebars), and if possible, brake in spurts rather than "dragging" them. On easy hills, practice using your brakes to get comfortable with them.

As was the case for steep uphills, steep descents require attention to weight distribution. Many riders lower their saddle an inch or two prior to descending (to get a lower center of gravity). All cyclists quickly learn to lift their weight slightly off the saddle and shift it back a few inches to keep traction and to avoid the feeling of being on the verge of catapulting over the handlebars. Practice this weight transfer on smooth but steep downhills so you can do it comfortably later on obstacle-laden terrain. Finally, it is possible to go too slow on a difficult downhill, so slow you can't "blast" over obstacles. Instead, because of lack of momentum, hazards can bring you to an abrupt stop or twist your front wheel, and both of these results can cause loss of control.

5. TURNING

A particularly treacherous time for mountain bikers is high speed or obstacle-laden turns. The first principle is: don't enter a curve too fast. Turns often contain loose dirt and debris created by all the mountain bikes that preceded you. Slow down before you get there; you can always accelerate during the turn if you choose. Lean around the turn as smoothly as possible, always keeping an eye out for obstacles. It is common for the rear wheel to skid in turns. To take the fright out of that phenomenon, go find a gentle turn with soft dirt and practice skidding to learn how you and your bike will respond.

6. OBSTACLES

If you get into the real spirit of off-road cycling, you will not ride just on smooth, groomed trails. You will encounter rocks, roots, limbs, logs, trenches, ruts, washboards, loose sand (or dirt or gravel), and water in a variety of forms from snow and ice to mud bogs to free-flowing springs and creeks. Obviously, the easiest means for handling an obstacle is to go around it; however, you can't always do that. For raised obstacles, those you need to get up and over, riders need to learn to "pop the front wheel." To practice this, find a low curb or set out a 4x4 piece of lumber. Approach it, and just before the front wheel impacts it, rapidly push down then pull up the front wheel. The wheel lift is enhanced if you simultaneously lower and raise your torso and apply a hard pedal stroke. After your front wheel clears the obstacle, shift your weight up and forward a little so the rear wheel can bounce over it lightly.

If you encounter "washboards," the key to relatively painless negotiating is to maintain a moderate speed and get into a shock absorbing posture— slightly up and off the saddle, knees slightly bent, elbows slightly bent, loose grip on the handlebars, and relaxed. Soft spots in the trail can make your bike difficult to control and create an instant slowdown. If you have to deal with loose, deep sand, dirt or gravel, the key is to go slower but "power through." Shift your weight back a little (for better traction), then keep your bike straight and keep pedaling. Maintaining momentum and a straight line is also important in mud holes; be certain to do any shifting prior to soft spots or muddy bogs (otherwise you will lose momentum). Sharp turns can present a particular problem in these conditions—you will be much more prone to losing the rear wheel to a slide out, so be extra cautious in sandy or muddy curves.

Going through water can be a lot of fun, or it can be a rude awakening if you find yourself upsidedown on a cold February afternoon. Before any attempt to cross a waterway, stop and examine it first. Make sure it isn't so deep that it will abruptly stop you, then find the route that has the fewest obstacles (look for deep holes, big rocks, and deep sand). Approach the crossing at a fairly low speed and plan on pedaling through it (rather than coasting) for maximum traction and control. Be aware of the potential for harmful effects that riding through water can have on your bearings (if they are not sealed) and exposed moving parts. Plan on lubricating your chain, derailleurs, inner wires, and so on, when you return home. Finally, regarding snow and ice, stay away from it as much as possible. Snow riding can be fun but if it's deep, it can be very laborious. Maintaining momentum and avoiding buried obstacles are the two major tasks for snow riders. Also, the difficulty of steep ascents and descents are significantly magnified by a few inches of snow. Most mountain bikers riding on snow prefer flat or nearly flat terrain.

R. W. Miskimins is the owner of Great Basin Bicycles in Reno, Nevada. He is the author of *Lake Tahoe's 20 Best Pavement and Dirt Rides, Guide 13— Reno/Carson Valley*, and coauthor of several other mountain bike guidebooks by Fine Edge Productions (see page 176).